Essential Histories

Genghis Khan & the
Mongol Conquests
1190–1400

Essential Histories

Genghis Khan & the Mongol Conquests 1190–1400

Stephen Turnbull

First published in Great Britain in 2003 by Osprey Publishing,
Midland House, West Way, Botley, Oxford OX2 0PH, UK
443 Park Avenue South, New York, NY 10016, USA
Email: info@ospreypublishing.com

ISBN-13 : 978-1-84176-523-5

A CIP catalogue record for this book is available from the British
Library

Editor: Sally Rawlings
Design: Ken Vail Graphic Design, Cambridge, UK
Cartography by The Map Studio
Index by Susan Williams
Origination by PPS Grasmere Ltd., Leeds, UK
Printed in China through Bookbuilders

Typeset in Monotype Gill Sans and ITC Stone Serif
08 09 10 11 12   16 15 14 13 12 11 10 9 8 7

For a complete list of titles available
from Osprey Publishing please contact:

NORTH AMERICA
Osprey Direct, C/o Random House Distribution Center,
400 Hahn Road, Westminster, MD 21157
E-mail: info@ospreydirect.com

ALL OTHER REGIONS
Osprey Direct UK, P.O. Box 140, Wellingborough,
Northants, NN8 2FA, UK
E-mail: info@ospreydirect.co.uk

www.ospreypublishing.com

Dedication

To my daughter Kate, for her 21st birthday.

Preface

This book provides a concise and reliable account of the vast
military enterprise known as the Mongol conquests from the
time of the unification of the Mongol tribes under Genghis Khan
to the death of his grandson, Khubilai Khan, a process that
encompassed almost exactly the entire 13th century of the
Christian era. A concluding section deals briefly with the
consequences arising out of the disintegration of the Mongol
Empire during the 14th century.

As the Mongol conquests were so far-ranging, descriptions of
their operations involve a considerable overlap of time. For this
reason I have organised 'The fighting' according to the particular
'theatre of war' where the Mongols were engaged. The reader is
referred to the chronology to see which parallel events were
taking place.

Acknowledgements

I have been very fortunate in that my travels over the past 30
years have allowed me to visit many of the places where the
Mongol conquests took place, and have been even more
fortunate to have friends who have visited other corners of the
far-flung Mongol Empire. Several of their excellent photographs
are included in this book. They include David Nicolle (Central
Asia), Thom Richardson (Syria), David Lambert and David Sneath
(Mongolia), William Lindesay (China), Peter Danford (Cambodia)
and Ian Clark (Poland). Till Weber kindly supplied me with his
own translation of the diary of a Jin official at the siege of Kaifeng
in 1232. I also thank everyone else who has helped me to gain
such a profound feeling for the sheer size of the Mongol
endeavours, an impression that I hope to convey to the reader
in the pages that follow. My wife, as usual, provided the
administrative back-up for the project.

Contents

Introduction

During the 13th century a military phenomenon arose in central Asia and provided the first instance in history of what was virtually a world war. From one side of the Euro/Asiatic land mass to the other, the fury of the Mongols exploded on to unsuspecting societies, most of which had previously been totally ignorant of the very existence of their new tormentors.

Among the few contemporary works of art that have survived to convey an impression of the appearance of these strange invaders are two objects that proclaim through very different cultural norms very similar images of the Mongol conquerors. At almost the

The Mongol warrior lies beneath the feet of Henry the Pious, killed at the battle of Leignitz, 1241. (Author's collection)

furthest point west reached by the Mongols lies Breslau (now Wroclaw in Poland) where lies buried Henry the Pious, Duke of Silesia, killed in battle with the Mongols at nearby Leignitz (Legnica) in 1241. Henry's tomb is now in the National Museum in Wroclaw, and beneath his feet lies a small carving of a Mongol warrior wearing the characteristic headgear.

Thirty years later and half a world away at the most easterly point of the Mongol conquests, an almost identical representation of Mongol warriors was being created. This time the image was not carved in stone but instead appeared on paper in a Japanese *emakimono* (horizontal picture scroll painting). The *Moko Shurai Ekotoba* (Mongol Invasion Scroll) was created not to remember a defeat, but to celebrate a victory, and in particular to press the claims for reward of the hero depicted therein: a leader of samurai called Takezaki Suenaga.

Neither Henry the Pious nor Takezaki Suenaga had the slightest idea that the other even existed, let alone that the two of them had fought a common enemy, but that was the nature of the Mongol Empire. Within the interval of time and space that lay between Leignitz and Hakata, the Mongols had fought battles in the deserts of Syria, skirmishes in the mountain passes of Afghanistan, sieges on the snowy plains of Russia and sea fights off the coast of Vietnam. Like a monstrous spider's web, the Mongol conquests affected the lives and livelihoods of countless peasants and kings.

The conquering Mongols were most feared by their victims as 'the devil's horsemen' who carried everything before them and left nothing behind. The devastation they caused will be noted frequently in the pages that follow, but one other feature that will be illustrated

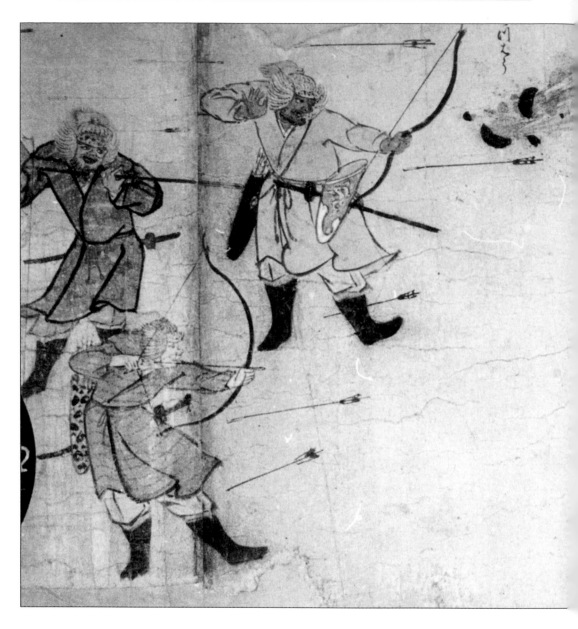

Half a world away from Poland, Mongol warriors were depicted on a Japanese *emakimono*. The *Moko Shurai Ekotoba* was created by Takezaki Suenaga to press his claims for reward after the war. (Author's collection)

throughout this work is the Mongols' amazing capacity to adapt to changed conditions and to learn new military techniques. This achievement is every bit as impressive as their traditional skills of mounted warfare.

We will also note that this achievement was not so evident during the early years of their conquests. The well-known comment that the Mongol Empire had been won on horseback but could not be governed from horseback referred to the administration of the conquered territories, but on several occasions it looked as though the Mongols could operate in no other way. Take away that vital element of mounted warfare and huge problems developed.

The greatest challenges to the apparently superhuman Mongols arose when they

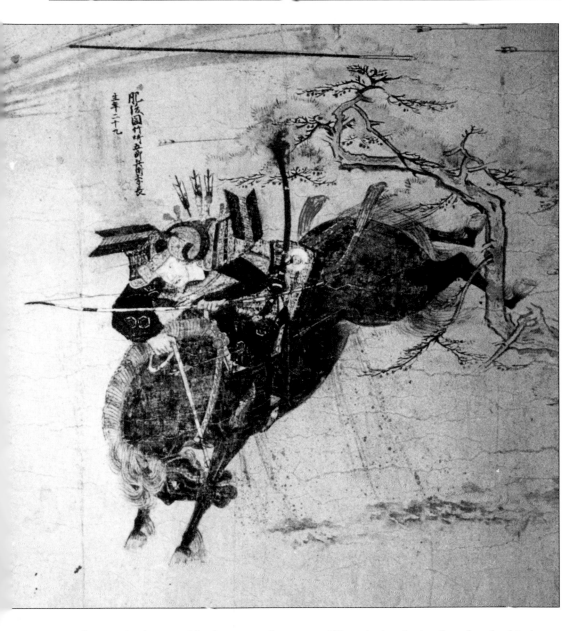

started campaigning outside the areas of steppe. The cultivated grain crops grown by sedentary societies were a good substitute for steppe grass for feeding their horses, but their exploitation required a different approach and needed considerable planning and forethought. Campaigns in unfamiliar temperatures and humidity or amid strange environments of swamp, jungle and wide rivers also provided battlegrounds that were very different from the familiar territory of the north. New military technologies therefore had to be learned and relearned. For example, when the Mongols marched against the Song in southern China from 1254 onwards they found that Song cities were both massive and very heavily defended. At Xiangyang in 1272 Khubilai Khan was forced to send to his kinsmen in the west for counterweight trebuchets, the latest thing in siege catapults, to breach its walls. The Mongols had this extraordinary ability to adapt and survive.

The Mongol Empire, 1190–1400

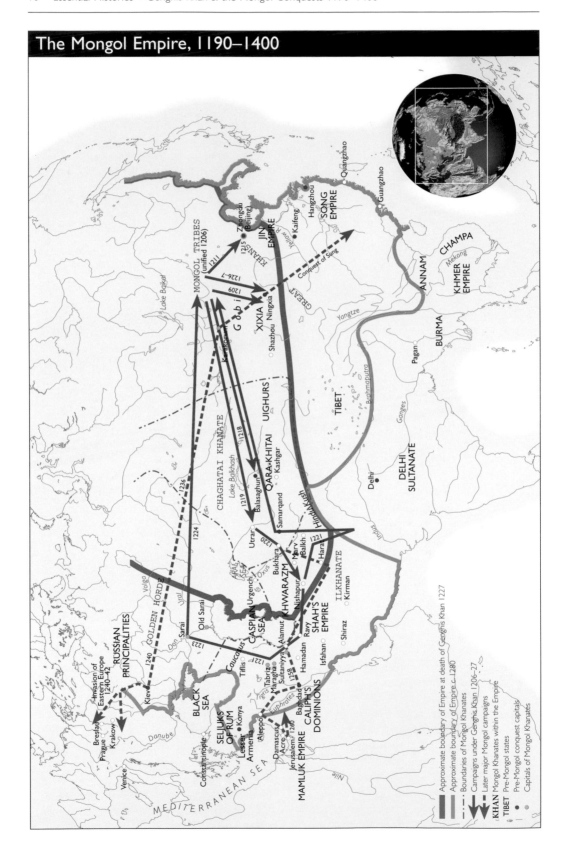

Chronology

1126 Jin dynasty captures Kaifeng from the Song dynasty
1167 Probable birth date of Temuchin (Genghis Khan)
1206 Temuchin is proclaimed universal Khan of all the Mongol tribes
1206 Mongol raids are conducted against the Xixia
1209 Xixia campaign begins; capture of Wolohai
1210 Surrender of Yinchuan
1211 Invasion of the Jin Empire by Genghis Khan
1212 Siege of Datong; Genghis Khan is wounded by an arrow
1213 Mongol attack on the Juyong Pass
1214 Siege of Ningjiang in Manchuria
1215 Capture of Zhongdu (Beijing)
1216 Mongols drive the Khitans into Korea
1218 Fall of Kashgar; Mongols defeat the Kara-Khitai
1219 Invasion of the Khwarazm Empire and the siege of Otrar; capture of Bukhara
1220 Capture of Samarkand
1221 Death of Shah Muhammad of Khwarazm; Genghis Khan's Afghan campaign begins; capture of Tirmiz, Balkh and Merv; capture of Nishapur
1222 Visit of the sage Changchun to Genghis Khan
1223 Battle of the Kalka river
1227 Second Xixia campaign begins; siege of Ningxia; death of Genghis Khan; death of Jochi
1231 Death of Jalal-al-Din; siege of Hezhong; siege of Kuju begins
1232 Siege of Kaifeng begins; Korean court moves to Kanghwa Island; Sartaq is killed at the siege of Ch'oin
1234 Suicide of the last Jin emperor
1235 The Great Kuriltai is held
1237 Invasion of northern Russian principalities begins; siege of Riazan
1238 Siege of Vladimir; battle of the Sit river
1239 Defeat of the Polovtsians (Cumans)

1240 Siege of Kiev (Kyiv)
1241 Battles of Cmielnik, Leignitz, Sajo river (Mohi); death of Ogodei Khan; Siege of Gran
1242 King Bela of Hungary flees to Croatia; Mongols leave Europe
1243 Submission of Prince Iaroslav Vsevolodich to the Golden Horde
1248 Death of Kuyuk Khan
1251 Carving of the *Tripitaka Koreana* completed; Mongke Khan launches the Persian campaign
1253 Siege of Ch'ungju; destruction of the Nanzhao kingdom at Dali
1254 Final Mongol invasion of Korea begins
1255 Death of Batu, khan of the Golden Horde
1256 Hulegu defeats the Ismailis (Assassins)
1257 Invasion of Annam
1258 Hulegu captures Baghdad
1259 Siege of Aleppo; death of Mongke Khan
1260 Accession of Khubilai Khan; Mongols defeated by Mamluks at Ain Jalut
1265 Battle of Daioyu. Mongols acquire a fleet; death of Hulegu, Ilkhan of Persia
1268 Siege of Xiangyang begins
1273 Peace settlement with Korea
1274 First invasion of Japan
1275 Bayan crosses the Yangtze
1277 Battle of Ngasaungyyan
1278 King of Champa pays homage to the Mongols
1279 Fall of the Southern Song
1281 Second invasion of Japan; Chams repudiate homage; invasion of Champa
1282 Mongol treaty of amity with Siam
1285 Battle of Siming
1287 Capture of Pagan; Capture of Hanoi
1288 Battle of the Bach Dang river
1293 Mongols land in Java
1294 Death of Khubilai Khan
1296 Mongol embassy to Cambodia
1301 Mongol attack on Lan Na; death of Kaidu
1356 Ming capture Nanjing
1368 Ming dynasty supplants the Yuan dynasty
1370 Death of the last Yuan emperor
1380 Battle of Kulikovo

The rise of the Mongols

The Mongols entered history as just one among a number of nomad tribes on the steppes of central Asia. As Juvaini puts it:

Before the appearance of Genghis Khan they had no chief or ruler. Each tribe or two tribes lived separately; they were not united with one another, and there was constant fighting and hostility between them. Some of them regarded robbery and violence, immorality and debauchery as deeds of manliness and excellence. The Khan of Khitai used to demand and seize goods from them. Their clothing was of the skins of dogs and mice, and their food was the flesh of those animals and other dead things. Their wine was mare's milk.

The rise of the Mongols and the beginnings of the Mongol conquests arose out of a dramatic shift from such disunity to unity, and it was achieved through the personality and military skills of one man. In all probability he was born in 1167. He was given the name of Temuchin.

The nomad world he entered was a fierce and unforgiving one of rivalry and survival skills. Like all Mongol children, Temuchin learned to ride with great skill and to handle a bow and arrows. After an eventful younger life his thoughts turned towards the

OPPOSITE Genghis Khan, who unified the Mongol tribes and created a world empire. (Author's collection)

BELOW The steppes of central Asia. (David Lambert)

opportunity of defeating his rivals and taking control of the unified Mongol tribes. Many years of warfare followed, the decisive victory being Temuchin's defeat of the Naimans. In 1206 a grand assembly was called at the source of the Onon river. A white standard symbolising the protective spirit of the Mongols was raised. Its nine points represented the newly unified Mongol tribes. The gathering then proclaimed Temuchin as Genghis Khan ('Universal Ruler').

The Xixia campaign 1205–10

When Temuchin accepted the title of Genghis Khan in 1206, his strategic needs changed – from unifying fiercely independent nomads to impressing them by demonstrating his power against the agriculture-based civilisations that bordered their lands. The first of these enemies lay nearby in China and, at that time, China was split under a number of different rulers whose distrust of one another made the prospect of their conquest look that much easier.

The two major power blocs in China at the beginning of the 13th century were the rival dynasties of the Jin and the Song. The Jin Empire lay to the north of the Yangtze river with its northern capital at Zhongdu, the site of present-day Beijing, while its southern capital was Kaifeng. The Jin were Jurchens, the same tribal peoples from Manchuria who would re-emerge centuries later as the Qing dynasty of China. During the 12th century the Jin had fought a long war against the Song dynasty, and in 1126 they had captured Kaifeng from the Song. From this time on, Song hegemony was confined to the area south of the Yangtze river, so that the dynasty became known as Southern Song. For a while they continued to fight back against the Jin and conducted operations from their new capital of Hangzhou from 1135 onwards.

In the north-west of China, however, there was another state called Xixia. They were Tangut people, and Genghis Khan

appreciated that the Xixia had to be his first objective because they could threaten his flank when he moved against the Jin. After a few exploratory raids in 1205 and 1206 Genghis Khan launched a major initiative in 1209 with the aim of completely destroying them. The operation began with a march of about 650 miles (1,000km), more than 200 miles (300km) of which was through the sandy wastes of the Gobi desert, and the Mongol army successfully stormed the Xixia fortress of Wolohai. The road ahead to the Xixia capital of Yinchuan lay over a high mountain range, and here the Xixia hit back. The result was a stalemate, but when further Tangut reinforcements arrived the Mongols deployed the tactic of a false withdrawal, a ruse that was to become a Mongol speciality, and succeeded in luring their opponents out of their fortified camp. A fierce battle ensued, during which the Xixia commander Weiming was captured.

Up to this point the traditional Mongol techniques of mobile cavalry tactics and a rapid assault on a fortified place had sufficed for victory to be gained, but the Xixia capital of Yinchuan had been prepared for a siege. The hitherto remorseless Mongol advance came to an abrupt halt in front of its walls and the complex system of irrigation canals around it that were fed from the Yellow river. For the first time in their history, the Mongols were confronted with the prospect of having to conduct a long siege against a fortified town. Their response to the challenge was a positive one and at Yinchuan we see an early example of the extraordinary skill the Mongols were to demonstrate throughout their campaigns of being able to learn and to adapt.

Seeing that the autumnal rains had swollen the Yellow river, Genghis Khan ordered the construction of a huge dyke. The river soon began to flood the city. Unfortunately for the Mongols, when the walls of Yinchuan were about to collapse in January 1210, the dyke burst. Whether or not it was the Xixia who caused the breach is not known, but the effect was to release a catastrophic flood against the Mongol siege lines. Nevertheless, the military

The Gobi desert. (David Lambert)

might that the Mongols had already demonstrated persuaded the Xixia ruler to submit. So he surrendered to Genghis Khan, flood or no flood. When he presented a lavish tribute to his conqueror, Genghis Khan withdrew, satisfied at the successful conclusion to his first operation against a sedentary civilised state.

The Kara-Khitai campaign

The minaret of the lost mosque at Uzgen at the eastern end of the Farghana valley (now in Kirghizstan). It dates from the 10th century. Uzgen was a major city in the Kara-Khitai state. (David Nicolle)

One of Genghis Khan's largest and most important military operations was directed against Islamic central Asia, and began with a useful but comparatively minor curtain-raiser – the conquest of the Kara-Khitai.

Following Genghis Khan's unification of the tribes, one of his enemies, Kuchlug of the Naimans, had escaped and taken refuge with the Gurkhan (ruler) of the Kara-Khitai, whose daughter he married. His father-in-law allowed him to gather Naiman tribesmen around him to form an army that would pose a threat to the security of the Mongol Empire, so in 1218 a Mongol corps of 20,000 men under Jebe appeared before Kashgar. The local population saw the Mongols as liberators from Kuchlug, so rebellion broke out, and Kuchlug was captured and killed. The Kara-Khitai lands were integrated into Mongol suzerainty.

The Mongol army

The army with which Genghis Khan had achieved supreme power among his own people was shortly to be unleashed upon their neighbours. The lighter Mongol cavalrymen wore sheepskin coats over their ordinary clothes, but recent research, including some very valuable archaeological finds, has demonstrated that a Mongol army would have consisted of a large number of heavy cavalrymen in addition to light cavalrymen. The armour that these horsemen wore was made in the common Asiatic style of lamellar armour, whereby small scales of iron or leather were pierced with holes and sewn together with leather thongs to make a composite armour plate. Alternatively, a heavy coat could be reinforced using metal plates. A coat was worn under the suit of armour, and heavy leather boots were worn on the feet. The helmet, which was made from a number of larger iron pieces, was roughly in the shape of a rounded cone, and had the added protective feature of a neck guard of iron plates. The Mongol heavy cavalry rode horses that also enjoyed the protection of lamellar armour. Bows, swords and maces were the main offensive weapons.

The organisation of the Mongol army

Mongol society, both civil and military (between which there was little distinction) was characterised by firm discipline. After visiting the Mongols in 1246, Giovanni di Piano Carpini wrote:

> The Tartars – that is, the Mongols – are the most obedient people in the world in regard to their leaders, more so even than our own clergy to their superiors. They hold them in the greatest reverence and never tell them a lie

At the apex of the Mongol social structure was the ruling Khan of the family of Genghis Khan, and the grazing lands allocated to Genghis Khan's four sons became the basis for the future khanates. This was the aristocracy of the steppes, a feudal structure found also in the army. A bond of personal loyalty linked the captains of tens (*arban*) with the captain of hundreds (*jaghun*), thousands (*mingghan*) and ten thousands (*tumen*), a simple decimal system that aided both delegation and communication. There was also an elite bodyguard for the Great Khan. In principle, the Mongol army was divided into three wings of left, right and centre, plus reserves.

Mongol campaign logistics

An army, said Napoleon, 'marches on its stomach', a celebrated dictum that has enshrined for ever in military history the importance of considering logistical matters when campaigns are being described. The supply and sourcing of food and water, the chains of command and of communication between the general and his lowliest foot soldier, the physical capabilities of the cavalry's mounts, the terrain to be covered – all are matters that require careful attention before drawing any conclusions about the course of an operation.

It is, however, noticeable that there is one army for whom such painstaking analysis is frequently abandoned. In the popular view, the Mongol armies of Genghis Khan and his successors stand alone in being spared from the harsh reality of campaign logistics. In this caricature, Mongol horsemen are invariably depicted as galloping everywhere.

They eat in the saddle, having tenderised their meat by making it into an extra layer of padding between man and horse. They fight in the saddle, dispatching clouds of arrows with great accuracy as they charge ahead; and then, when exhausted by these endeavours, they even sleep in the saddle as their mounts carry them unerringly towards their next encounter.

This larger-than-life image must certainly have been the impression given to the Mongols' victims during their great conquests, and one can easily imagine a central Asian peasant standing in bemused terror as a horde of mounted demons suddenly appear out of nowhere to destroy utterly the world he has known. There is also considerable evidence that the Mongols deliberately fostered this superhuman image to help their campaigns along, until the cumulative effect of their unstoppable reputation led some cities to surrender without putting up any resistance. But if medieval peasants could be fooled into thinking that the Mongols were superhuman, the same should not be said for modern historians. Yet time and again we meet the same assumptions of immense speed and complete independence from conventional logistics, whereby the armies are portrayed in an almost endless charge, sustained only on mare's milk and horse blood.

Needless to say, the Mongols themselves were under no illusions about logistical reality. Each man kept a string of 16 horses, not just one or two, a huge asset to mobility that arose out of their nomadic background. The addition of another two horses to this total to provide meat on the hoof would have kept a Mongol army in the field for about six months without cutting appreciably its rate of movement, leaving the milk and the blood for emergency situations.

Yet the rate of travel of a Mongol army was by no means as rapid as is popularly assumed. During the campaigns in China against the Jin Empire the Mongols travelled on average only up to about 14 miles (23km)

a day. This was because the immense logistical advantage they gained from the horses' ability to live off the pasture lands over which they rode had a limitation in that the horses had to have time to graze, a process that takes longer than feeding horses with fodder. Nevertheless, it was this factor, which derived directly from the nature of life on the steppes from which they had come, that allowed the initially remorseless spread of the Mongol conquests.

The enemies of the Mongols

So far-reaching were the Mongol conquests that they fought a larger variety of enemy than any army in history. Some were nomads like themselves who relied on swift light cavalry. Others were sedentary societies who took refuge behind heavy armour or city walls.

The easiest target for the Mongols would appear to have been European heavy cavalry. The Mongol never placed themselves in a position where a charge by mounted knights could hurt them. At Leignitz and Mohi, clever Mongol tactics neutralised the better defensive armour possessed by the knights.

China produced a multitude of challenges, and for much of their history the Chinese seem to have had the technological edge over the Mongols. The Chinese were the first to use exploding gunpowder bombs. The first type to be devised were soft-cased 'thunderclap bombs'. These were followed by iron 'thunder crash bombs' or 'heaven shaking thunder' as they were sometimes known, which killed people by the shattering of their metal cases and destroyed objects by the increased force of the explosion that is implied by the dramatically enhanced name. They were shaped like a bottle gourd with a small opening, and were made from cast iron about 5cm (2 inches) thick. The fragments produced when the bombs exploded caused great personal injury, and one Southern Song officer was blinded in an explosion that also wounded half a dozen other men.

Their first recorded use in war dates from the siege by the Jin of the Southern Song city of Qizhou in 1221.

Land mines were also used against the Mongols as the Song fought to the last man. The simplest sort were just large explosive bombs placed at a spot where one's enemy was expected, and then detonated using some form of time fuse. A dramatic incident involving just such a planned delayed explosion occurred in 1277 at Guilin in Guangxi province, one of the last outposts of Southern Song resistance to the Mongols. When the main citadel fell, a truce was arranged so that the garrison could receive supplies prior to an honourable surrender. During the interregnum some Mongol soldiers climbed up on to the now undefended walls, when suddenly there was an enormous explosion which brought down the wall and the Mongols with it. The Southern Song defenders had prepared a huge bomb at its foundations, and had ignited it at just the right moment.

The Koreans made use of more primitive siege weaponry, throwing molten iron projectiles at the Mongols. But one other means of Korean resistance was used for the first time during the third invasion of Korea. This was guerrilla warfare, conducted by the Korean *py'olch'o* (patrols). They laid ambushes for Mongol columns and fought small-scale skirmishes. They also raided Mongol camps, taking many heads and much plunder. This proved to be a very effective way of harassing the invading armies.

Unlike the Koreans, the Japanese seem to have suffered a remarkable culture shock when the Mongols launched their surprise invasion. At first the samurai tried to fight back using their traditional techniques. Their ideal of martial behaviour was still that of the individual and elite mounted archer testing his skills against a worthy opponent summoned by issuing a challenge. The great difficulty that the Mongol invasion produced for the samurai was the impossibility of communicating challenges to an opponent who did not speak Japanese. As the *Hachiman Gudokun* relates:

According to our manner of fighting we must first call out by name someone from the enemy ranks, and then attack in single combat. But they took no notice at all of such conventions. They rushed forward all together in a mass, grappling with any individuals they could not catch and killing them.

The Mongols' advance and withdrawal to the accompaniment of drums, bells and shouted war-cries alarmed the Japanese horses. The samurai were also faced with a different archery technique, whereby arrows were shot in huge clouds, rather than being used in long-range individual combat. Dense showers of arrows, some tipped with poison, were poured into the Japanese lines. Any individual combats that did take place were anonymous affairs, although there are several accounts of samurai attempting to seek out high-ranking Mongol warriors.

In Burma the Mongol horses were startled by Burmese war elephants, but as on so many other occasions the Mongols refused to be panicked and calmly dismounted. They first took their mounts to the rear and then returned to loose arrows against the elephants. This action stampeded them, leading to a great Mongol victory.

The Chinese chronicles of the Mongol conquest of Java tell us little about the weapons used by the Javanese, but later Javanese epics, written during the 16th century about events during the 14th century, enable us to make some educated guesses about the warriors who faced the Mongols. There would almost certainly have been only a few elephants, as the elephant is not a native of Java, and senior commanders would have reserved any for their own use. One novelty inflicted on the Mongols would have been darts from blowpipes, a weapon noted on other occasions. Finally, the invaders would have been subject to that apparently uncontrolled and frenzied attack characteristic of the area, carried out like a forlorn hope unit composed of crazed fanatics, the description of which has entered our language as 'running amok'.

Beyond the steppes

The Khwarazm campaign

The Mongol campaigns of conquest may be said to have begun when Genghis Khan turned his attentions away from his immediate neighbours towards less familiar foes. He began with the conquest of the Khwarazm Empire.

The success of the Kara-Khitai operation brought Genghis Khan into close proximity with the man who was to become one of his most serious rivals: the Shah (or Sultan) Muhammad of Khwarazm, who controlled most of the eastern Muslim world. The Khwarazm Shah was from a Turkic family and ruled a recently integrated but heterogeneous empire stretching from the Aral Sea to the Persian Gulf, and including Afghanistan and the whole of Iran. There were profound divisions among the Shah's subjects and also among his high officials, and these produced such mistrust that the Shah was reluctant to entrust the command of his army to one man, lest a victor become

a future rival. All these were weaknesses that Genghis Khan was determined to exploit.

In 1219 Genghis Khan launched a major campaign against Muhammad, the pretext for the invasion being the Shah's treatment of Muslim merchants under Mongol protection, whom he accused of spying. But the trigger to immediate action was the execution of some Mongol envoys. According to the historian Juvaini, when Genghis Khan learned of the massacre he climbed to the top of a hill, uncovered his head and prayed to heaven for three days 'for the strength to exact vengeance'.

Before leaving on campaign Genghis Khan settled the matter of his own succession by naming Ogodei as his heir, and spent the summer of 1219 conducting

The Farghana valley viewed from Osh (now the eastern-most tip of Uzbekistan). Jochi made a feint attack into the Farghana valley from Kashgar before the main attack on Khwarazm in 1219. (David Nicolle)

The late 9th- or early 10th-century brick mausoleum of Ismail, founder of the Samanid dynasty at Bukhara, one of the few buildings to survive the Mongol onslaught. (David Nicolle)

military manoeuvres and arranging provisions. In the autumn of that year the Mongols approached the city of Otrar, Genghis Khan's arrival being preceded by propaganda and proclamations that made the most of the division within the Shah's supporters. Otrar fell after a five-month siege, the final defence being conducted by die-hards who flung down roof tiles on to the heads of the besiegers. The governor was executed, but the dramatic legend of his death – Genghis Khan is said to have had molten silver poured into his ears and eyes – is probably a fabrication.

While the siege was still in progress, the confident Genghis Khan left a section of his army in charge of the Otrar lines and moved across the desert towards his next objective: Bukhara. This city had only been part of the Khwarazm Empire since 1207, and on the approach of the Mongols as many as 20,000 men of the garrison fled from their posts, leaving only 500 Turkish troops behind, barricaded in the citadel. They were easily overcome.

The next Mongol objective was Samarkand, which, although having a large army to defend it, suffered from the same political divisions and rivalries that plagued the whole of the Khwarazm Empire. A brave sortie from the city was attempted by Turkish troops using elephants, but the Mongols dealt with this by their well-honed tactic of using mounted archery to break up an enemy formation. Juvaini colourfully describes the operation as being like a game of chess:

And when the path of combat was closed to them, and the two parties had become entangled on the chess board of war, and the valiant knights were no longer able to manoeuvre their horses upon the plain, they threw in their elephants; but the Mongols did not turn tail, on the contrary, with their King-checking arrows they liberated those who were held in check by the elephants and broke up the ranks of the infantry. When the elephants had received wounds and were of no more use than the foot soldiers of chess, they turned back, tramping many people underneath their feet.

The Mongols then broke through the walls and began to pillage Samarkand, guaranteeing safety to anyone who put up no resistance and did not attempt to conceal himself. Anyone who disobeyed this command and was found hiding in a cellar was killed on the spot.

The mahouts brought their elephants to Genghis Khan and demanded elephant fodder. He asked them what the elephants lived on before they fell into captivity. They replied, 'the grass of the plains', whereupon he ordered the elephants to be set free to forage for themselves. They were accordingly released and finally perished from hunger.

All that was left to resist Genghis Khan was the determined garrison inside the citadel. The Mongols captured the gates 'between the two prayers' and:

A thousand brave and valiant men withdrew to the cathedral mosque and commenced a fierce battle using both naphtha and quarrels. The army of Genghis Khan likewise employed pots of naphtha; and the Friday mosque and all that were in it were burnt with the fire of this world and washed with the water of the hereafter.

OPPOSITE The minaret at Vabkant between Bukhara and Samarkand is one of the few monuments to have survived the Mongol attack undamaged. It was built in 1196. (David Nicolle)

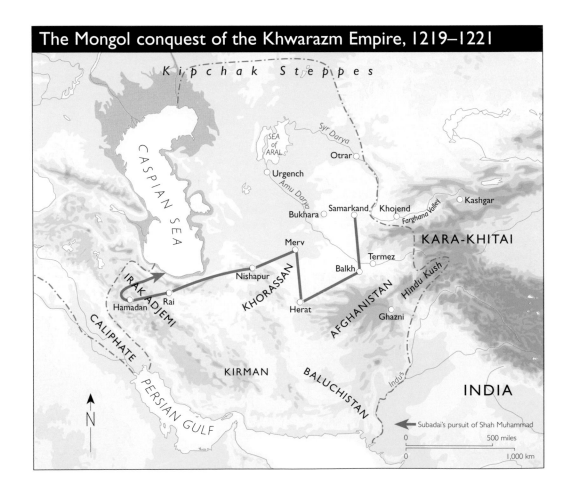

The Mongol conquest of the Khwarazm Empire, 1219–1221

Kipchak Steppes

CASPIAN SEA

SEA of ARAL

Syr Darya

Otrar

Urgench

Amu Darya

Samarkand   Khojend   Kashgar

Bukhara   Farghana Valley

KARA-KHITAI

Merv

Termez

Nishapur   Balkh   Hindu Kush

IRAK ADJEMI   KHORASSAN

Rai   Herat   AFGHANISTAN

Hamadan   Ghazni

CALIPHATE

KIRMAN   BALUCHISTAN   Indus   INDIA

PERSIAN GULF

N

Subadai's pursuit of Shah Muhammad

0   500 miles

0   1,000 km

Old Samarkand, which was abandoned after the Mongol Conquest. (David Nicolle)

A delegation of senior clerics then opened negotiations with Genghis Khan. They and their followers were guaranteed their lives and were driven out of the city. Three hundred craftsmen from their number were taken into Mongol service, and the rest were permitted to return to their devastated homes.

The fall of Samarkand decided the outcome of the Khwarazm war. The old capital of Khwarazm, Urgench on the Amu Darya river, fell after a long siege, so the Khwarazm Shah became a fugitive after nominating his son, Jalal al-Din, as his successor. Genghis Khan resolved to destroy the son, and left the pursuit of the former Shah Muhammad to his two best generals, Jebe and Subadai. The old Shah certainly kept his Mongol pursuers busy, but eventually died of pneumonia in 1221 on an island in the Caspian Sea.

Genghis Khan's Afghan war

Meanwhile Genghis Khan took personal command of the operation that went in pursuit of the new Sultan Jalal al-Din. He had left for Afghanistan, where he hoped to organise a new army to fight back against the Mongols. Genghis Khan crossed the Amu Darya in 1221 and took Tirmiz (the modern Termez, where the river Oxus forms the boundary between Uzbekistan and Afghanistan) with much slaughter, and then captured Balkh. These places appear to have received much more systematic destruction than Samarkand and Bukhara. The next to fall was Merv, where the Mongol general Tolui is said to have sat on a golden chair to watch the execution of the population. According to tradition, it was as a result of the sack of Merv that a certain Oghuz tribe whose grazing grounds were in the near vicinity emigrated to the safety of Asia Minor where the Seljuks gave them land, a move that became the foundation of the Ottoman Empire.

The subsequent Mongol attack on Nishapur provides us with more details about Mongol warfare, and much more evidence of a harsher treatment of a defeated population. This was partly because during a preliminary attack an arrow killed Genghis Khan's son-in-law, Toghachar. When the Mongols returned they came well prepared for a long siege and were keen to take a ruthless revenge. We read that:

although Nishapur is in a stony region they loaded stones at a distance of several stages and brought them with them. These were piled up like heaps in a harvest, and not a tenth part of them was used. The people of Nishapur saw that the matter was serious and that these were not the same men they had seen before; and although they had three thousand crossbows in action on the wall and had set up three hundred mangonels and ballistas and laid in a corresponding quantity of missiles and naphtha, their feet were loosened and they lost heart.

When the Mongols entered Nishapur a thirst for vengeance arising out of Toghachar's death made the sack all the more terrible:

They then drove all the survivors, men and women, out on to the plain; and in order to avenge Toghachar it was commanded that the town should be laid waste in such a manner that the site could be ploughed upon; and that in the exaction of vengeance not even cats and dogs should be left alive.

Genghis Khan's son Tolui then went on to take Herat, and eventually rejoined his father near Thaleqan. However, Jalal-al-Din, the object of their destructive attentions, had managed to slip through the Mongols' vast cordon and had disappeared into the wild mountains of Afghanistan. Here he took refuge in Ghazni, in the heart of the Afghan wilderness, where he organised a new army and managed to defeat a small Mongol force sent against him near Kabul.

Urgench, one of the biggest cities in central Asia, was the old capital of the Shah of Khwarazm. (David Nicolle)

Intent on finding and destroying the fugitive, the Mongols pursued him from valley to valley. Forced marches eventually brought the Mongol army within sight of his army on the bank of the Indus river just as Jalal al-Din was about to cross it. Encircled by Mongol horsemen, Jalal al-Din was forced to fight, and when his army was destroyed he swam his horse to the far bank. Genghis Khan, who admired his skills and fortitude, let him go, whereupon the hero sought refuge in the court of the Sultan of Delhi. Jalal al-Din kept up the struggle against the Mongols for many years until being murdered in 1231.

The war in Afghanistan was virtually over when Genghis Khan received news of a rebellion by the Xixia. He first intended to return home via India, but the natural obstacles and the unfamiliarity with the terrain made him choose the Afghanistan route instead. This took him back over the scenes of his earlier triumphs, where any rekindled resistance was harshly dealt with. Balkh, for example, suffered an almost unique second wave of terror when the Mongols returned. Juvaini tells us:

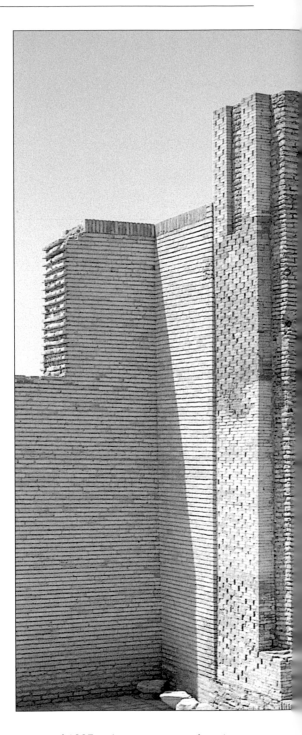

> When Genghis Khan returned from Peshawar and arrived at Balkh, he found a number of fugitives who had remained hidden in nooks and crannies and had come out again. He commanded them all to be killed, and fulfilled upon them the verse, 'Twice we will chastise them.' And wherever a wall was left standing, the Mongols pulled it down and for a second time wiped out all traces of culture from that region.

Genghis Khan stayed for some time in Afghanistan south of the Hindu Kush, and it was there that he received in audience the renowned Chinese sage Changchun, (whose story is related on page 80). He wintered in Samarkand and spent the spring of 1223 north of the Syr Darya, probably near Tashkent. When he arrived back in Mongolia in 1225 Genghis Khan turned his attentions once again to the Xixia, who provided his last campaign. In the spring of 1227 a siege commenced against Ningxia, where:

> In vain the inhabitants hid in mountains and caves to escape the Mongol might. The fields were covered with human bones.

Nevertheless Ningxia held out, and while the siege was still continuing Genghis Khan died in his military camp on 18 August 1227. Soon afterwards Ningxia fell, and in accordance with the world conqueror's last wishes, all its inhabitants were put to the

This building in Urgench is believed to have been the palace of Shah Muhammad of Khwarazm. (David Nicolle)

sword. The Great Khan was dead, but his successors were to continue his work for the next 80 years.

Building an empire

The northern Chinese theatre 1211–34

The Khwarazm campaign had thus launched Genghis Khan on to the world stage, but we must now backtrack a little to pick up on the progress that was being made in the Mongol conquest of China, the operation that had begun with the first Xixia campaign.

The process by which Genghis Khan and his successors took over the whole of China from the Jin and the Song dynasties and set up their own Yuan (Mongol) dynasty was the longest campaign of all the military actions involved in creating their spectacular empire. It began with Genghis Khan's operation against the Xixia and was only completed 70 years later by his grandson Khubilai Khan, the first Yuan emperor of China. Almost all the other Mongol operations, from Syria to Poland and from Russia to Japan, were carried out against the backdrop of this long struggle for China. Within that period of time the Mongols fought on grasslands, in sub-tropical jungles, in deserts, across temperate farmlands, along rivers and on the sea, just to subdue that one enormous and complex country. The campaign also spanned an enormous conceptual gap that reached from nomadism to imperialism, and was symbolised by the difference between the dwelling of the first Mongol leader, who lived in a portable felt tent, and that of his grandson, who owned the palace now known to the popular imagination as Xanadu.

The advance against the Jin
When the Mongols besieged Yinchuan in 1209 the Xixia had requested help from the Jin. None came, and when the victorious Mongols had barely departed, the angry Xixia made a raid over the border into Jin territory, thus breaking a truce that had existed between them since 1165. Needless to say, such rash behaviour simply played into the Mongols' hands.

Soon after his return to Mongolia from Yinchuan, Genghis Khan received word that

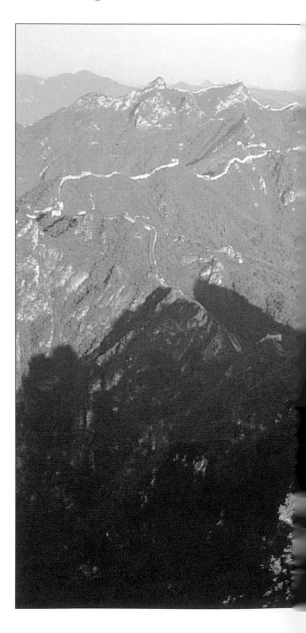

a new Jin emperor had succeeded to the throne. The emperor expected the Mongol ruler, as his traditional but nominal vassal, to formally acknowledge his suzerainty. But times had changed. Instead of bowing, Genghis Khan turned to the south and spat on the ground as a gesture of defiance. War with the Jin was now inevitable.

The previous Jin emperor had long been concerned about the Mongol threat and had strengthened his north-western border with a line of fortifications connected by walls and ditches. But when Genghis Khan moved against them in 1211, this border line, the Jin contribution to what we now call the Great Wall of China, proved hopelessly ineffective. The Mongols moved on two fronts, separated sometimes by over 200 miles (320km), but kept in constant communication with each

A panoramic view of the Great Wall of China. This section, built under the Ming, did not exist when the Mongols invaded China, but would not have been very effective in keeping them away. (William Lindesay)

The Mongol conquest of China and Korea, 1211–1273

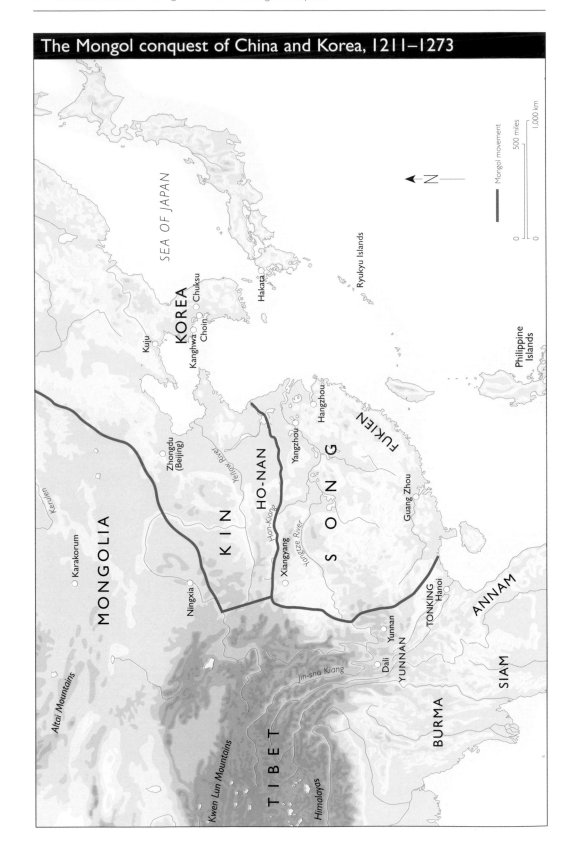

other through highly mobile scouts. Genghis Khan took personal command of the eastern army and headed for the strategic Juyong Pass, which protected Zhongdu (Beijing) from the north. The Jin tried to strengthen their defences by fortifying the pass, but Jebe, the leader of the Mongol vanguard, overcame all resistance. The main body then descended into the plains around Beijing, where they plundered extensively, but made no attempt to besiege the capital at that stage.

During the winter of 1211 the Mongols withdrew. This gave the Jin an opportunity to reorganise, but the Khan's army returned in 1212. This time Genghis Khan advanced against the Jin's western capital at modern Datong in Shanxi province, and was severely wounded by an arrow. He had with him a Chinese renegade called Liu Po-lin who was an expert at siegecraft. His presence was evidence of the Mongols' willingness to learn from their enemies. But Datong had still not fallen by the time the Mongols withdrew to their winter quarters,

In 1213 another Mongol incursion headed once again for the Juyong Pass, which the Jin had reinforced with elite troops. According to some reports the gates were sealed with iron and the surrounding country for 30 miles (50km) around was scattered with iron caltrops. The Jin resistance was so firm that it forced the Mongols into a large detour to find another pass. More raids and plunder followed through an extensive operation involving highly mobile yet co-ordinated advances, one of which (under Mukhali) reached Fengzhou and gave the Mongols their first sight of the sea. Their newly acquired expertise in siegecraft also played its part, and we find the Mongols making use of the unusual siege weapon of incendiaries conveyed by expendable birds at the siege of Ningjiang in Manchuria in 1214.

Great progress was made, and by early 1214, according to a Chinese historian, 'everywhere north of the Yellow river there could be seen dust and smoke, and the sound of drums rose to Heaven'. Much of the Jin Empire was now in Mongol hands,

and Beijing was surrounded. Other towns and cities had fallen, partly because of siege weapons but also as a result of ruthless intimidation. As they passed through outlying districts of fortified places the Mongols rounded up thousands of captives. After these unfortunates had been forced to erect siegeworks they were made to lead assaults as human shields. Often, we are told, the besieged citizens recognised their relatives in the vanguard of the storming party and refused to fight, thus giving the Mongols an easy victory.

On one occasion the reports of the Mongols' growing prowess with catapults ensured that the inhabitants of a city targeted for attack not only laid waste the countryside for 4–5 miles (6–8 km) around, but also carefully removed every stone they could find so that these could not be used as catapult ammunition. There was a similar shortage of stones during another campaign. We are not told whether this was deliberate, but the Mongol artillerymen instead used balls of mulberry wood, hardened by soaking them in water. We also read of the Mongols digging a mine under the Xixia fortress of Shazhou in 1224. Nothing seems to have been beyond their capabilities.

The fall of Beijing

Alarmed by these developments, the Jin emperor decided to move his court to their southern capital at Kaifeng which was protected to the north by the Yellow river. Here he would plan a counter-offensive. Genghis Khan interpreted this move as a preparation for war, so he decided to redouble his efforts against Zhongdu (Beijing). Even in China, a land of great cities, the walls of Zhongdu were considered very large and its defences exceptional. The walls, which were built of stamped clay and crowned with crenellated brick battlements, measured 18 miles (28km) in circumference and reached a height of 12m (40 feet). Twelve gates gave access to the city, and there were 900 towers and three lines of moats. Several Mongol assaults failed, so the decision was made to let starvation do the work for them.

The Juyong Pass, through which the Mongols invaded the Jin Empire, as seen from the modern road to Beijing. (William Lindesay)

By the summer of 1215 there were reports of cannibalism, and in June the Jin commander abandoned his post and fled to join the emperor in Kaifeng. The city surrendered soon afterwards, and was thoroughly sacked and burned. The fall of Zhongdu marked the real beginning of the Mongol domination of China. A disinterested and therefore unbiased eye-witness reported several months later that the bones of the slaughtered formed white mountains and that the soil was still greasy with human fat.

The death of Genghis Khan in 1227 gave the Jin a brief respite from Mongol attentions. But in 1230 his successor, Ogodei, began a large-scale operation against them, and the year 1231 was to find the Jin besieged by a Mongol army in Hezhong and using the iron bombs described above to defend themselves. When the city fell, the Jin escaped along the Yellow river, and we are told that they fired iron thunder crash bombs at the Mongol boats attempting to delay their progress, and broke through the cordon.

The great siege of Kaifeng

The year 1232 saw the celebrated siege of the Jin's former southern (and now their only remaining) capital at Kaifeng by the Mongols under the famous general Subadai. We know quite a lot about the siege from a fascinating and graphic description of life in the besieged capital that was compiled by a Jin official. He wrote that Kaifeng had been in a state of shock as the Mongols approached, because their arrival was preceded by bad news of Jin defeats in the northern mountains where the soldiers were in snow up to their knees. After one encounter a Jin commander had been discovered hiding in a hole in the ground and had been killed.

To raise the morale in Kaifeng the emperor deliberately made himself highly visible to his troops by touring the walls as the Mongol bombardment began. At this stage in their development the Mongols do not appear to have possessed any exploding bombs of their own, and their trebuchet missiles, flung from simple traction trebuchets operated by crews of hauliers, were confined to large stones 'like half millstones'. They were nonetheless very effective, and the account then tells us:

The northern [Mongol] army intensified the bombardment of the city and the stone balls flew in like rain showers. The crews [of the city's own artillery] were put in terrible confusion and were partly crushed, partly pounded.

However, the Jin could hit back with exploding bombs, and:

The heavy pieces in the city – they were called 'heaven shaking thunder' – replied.

Wherever the northern army was hit fires started that burned many people to cinders.

Another account gives more detail about how the thunder crash bombs were actually used. The fuses were lit, the trebuchets' ropes were pulled and:

There was a great explosion, the noise whereof was like thunder, audible for more than a hundred li, and the vegetation was scorched and blasted by the heat over an area of more than half a mou. When hit, even iron armour was quite pierced through. Those who were not wounded by fragments were burned to death by the explosions.

Faced with these devastating weapons, the Mongol assault parties were forced to resort to desperate protective measures as they approached the city walls:

Therefore the Mongol soldiers made cowhide shields to cover their approach trenches and men beneath the walls, and dug as it were niches, each large enough to contain a man, hoping that in this way the troops above would not be able to do anything about it. But someone suggested the technique of lowering the thunder crash bombs on iron chains. When these reached the trenches where the Mongol were making their dugouts, the bombs were set off, with the result that the cowhide and the attacking soldiers were all blown to bits, not even a trace being left behind.

Another weapon used by the Jin was the fire lance, which consisted of an ordinary spear to which was affixed a tube rather like a roman candle. It was lit by means of glowing tinder carried in a box at the soldier's belt and burned for about five minutes. When it was burned out its operator could use the spear for its conventional purpose. At Kaifeng we read that:

... the defenders had at their disposal flying-fire spears. These were filled with gunpowder, and, when ignited, flames shot

forwards for a distance of more than ten paces, so that no one dared come near. These thunder crash bombs and flying-fire spears were the only two weapons that the Mongol soldiers were really afraid of.

In spite of the Jin's undoubted technical superiority in matters of explosives, the situation in Kaifeng rapidly deteriorated. An edict was therefore issued by the Jin emperor conscripting all males for the defence of the town walls on pain of death. Even the bookish students of Kaifeng, whom the government had decided were too weak for actual fighting, were eventually drafted into the trebuchet crews. Yet even this was too strenuous a prospect for some of them, and they petitioned the emperor to allow them to provide administrative support instead. Some got what they wanted, and the account continues:

Furthermore, he ordered them to climb to the walls and let paper kites fly on which they had to fix a text asking the section of the population that had been forced to collaborate with the enemy outside to escape and return to the city in order to collect an official reward. Doing all these tasks the students could not avoid being exposed to the enemy's arrows and stone balls. Also, he made the students pull up the signal lanterns which signalled the start of sorties through the secret gates at night. If a lantern went out, the man responsible for it was executed. The students felt very bitter about this treatment.

A different account tells us that the string of the kites was cut so that they fell among the Mongol lines like a leaflet raid, but the Mongol besiegers scorned the whole process.

During the winter, the Jin emperor, who had previously fled from Beijing, took the opportunity to flee from Kaifeng while he still had the chance. This caused such a catastrophic drop in morale that the officers left behind decided to surrender to avoid a

OPPOSITE Rebuilding a section of the Great Wall above the Juyong Pass. (William Lindesay)

worse sack than could be expected if the city was taken by storm. It was a wise decision, and after some slaughter the Mongols pursued the Jin emperor to nearby Caizhou where he had taken refuge. The Jin dynasty came to an end when he committed suicide in 1234.

Looking northwards from behind their supposed barrier of the Yangtze, members of the Southern Song dynasty smirked as they contemplated the destruction of the northern upstarts who had once humiliated them, but as an ambassador from the Jin reminded them, they now had an even worse neighbour to fear. It was not many years before the Southern Song discovered exactly what he meant.

The Korean theatre 1216–73

Throughout its entire history the fate of the Korean peninsula has been closely tied to developments in China, and the history of the Mongol conquests is no exception. The first military contacts between the Mongols and Korea came about as a result of the Mongols' defeat of the Khitans, a people of the same ethnic stock as the Kara-Khitai, whose Liao dynasty of China had previously succumbed to the Jin. In 1216 the Mongols drove the Khitans to the Yalu river, which was, and still is, the border with Korea. When the Koreans refused them supplies, the Khitans crossed the border to pillage and occupy towns, so Korea was forced to fight back against them.

The first Mongol invasion of Korea

During the winter of 1216 the Mongols invaded Korea in pursuit of the Khitans. They first met resistance at the walled city of Kangdong. A heavy fall of snow cut the roads to the Mongols' rear, and encouraged the Khitans to think that they could hold out until a lack of supplies forced the Mongols to retreat. The Mongol response was to ask the Korean government of the Koryo dynasty to assist them on the grounds that they had come to Korea to liberate its people from the Khitan yoke.

The Koryo rulers were very hesitant about co-operating with 'the most inhuman of northern barbarians' as one perceptive courtier described the Mongols. When agreement was given the Korean commander Cho Ch'ung proceeded with great caution, merely sending his general Kim Ingyong to the Mongols with some supplies. Kim was also ordered to keep the Mongol operation under close observation and at Taech'on the archers in his army made a gesture of assisting in the reduction of this Khitan-held fortress. In 1219 a large Korean army joined the Mongols in a more serious effort aimed at the reduction of Khitan-occupied Kangdong. The walls were completely surrounded by the allied armies and 40 Khitans came out to surrender. Feeling abandoned, the Khitan leader hanged himself.

With their immediate objectives satisfied the Mongols left Korea, having first demanded an enormous tribute from the Koryo leaders whom their intervention had supposedly saved. The mistrustful Koreans were quite sure that the Mongols would return. Indeed, some Mongols had not quite left Korea, but had settled in the border town of Uiju with instructions 'to practise the language of Koryo and wait for our return'.

The second Mongol invasion of Korea

The uneasy peace lasted until 1225, enlivened by periods of tension when envoys came to collect tribute, and then a very serious incident severely tested Koryo–Mongol relations. A Korean account tells how:

The Mongol envoys left the Western capital (P'yongyang) and crossed the Yalu. Of the national gifts which had been presented, they kept only the otter pelts, and as regards the remainder, that is, the silks and so on, they abandoned them in the fields. On the way back they were killed by bandits. The Mongols suspected us. Therefore, relations were broken off.

It was only the pressure on Mongol military resources elsewhere that prevented

In August 1232 Sartaq swept southwards into the Han river valley and besieged a small mountain fortress called Ch'oin. He was killed by a Korean arrow. (Author's collection)

another invasion of Korea from happening there and then, and it was not until 1231 that the Mongols again crossed the Yalu. By this time Korea had aroused further Mongol anger by refusing to help them in their campaign against the Jin. So in August of that year a large Mongol force under General

Sartaq laid siege to Uiju. The garrison soon surrendered, and the Mongols headed south to besiege Kuju, a city that was to become famous in the annals of siege warfare when it experienced one of the longest and best-recorded sieges of all the Mongols' conquests. General Kim Ch'ungon defended the eastern and western walls, while Kim Kyongson held the southern part. They were both under the overall command of the heroic Pak So:

When the Mongols arrived with a large force at the southern gate of the city, Kyongson leading his twelve soldiers as well as the patrols of all the cities, ordered the soldiers as they were going out of the city gate, 'Do not think of your own lives. If fate decrees, die, but do not fall back.' The patrols then threw themselves on the ground and would not obey. Kyongson ordered them all to go back into the city and then with only his twelve soldiers he advanced into battle. Kim himself shot an arrow and knocked down one mounted soldier who rode with a black flag in the vanguard. Consequently Kim's twelve soldiers were encouraged and fought strenuously. Hit by an arrow, Kyongson's arm was dripping wet with blood. Still, he pressed his men forward without stopping. Battle was joined four or five times and the Mongols withdrew.

The siege continued with furious Mongol attacks against Kuju's walls. They loaded carts with grass and wood and overturned them beside the gates so that fires could be started. They built siege towers and used hide-covered 'sows' to protect parties digging under the walls. The Korean defenders responded by bombarding the Mongol assault parties with molten iron projectiles flung by traction trebuchets, throwing burning straw at the siege towers and countermining the tunnellers.

Sartaq sent the Koryo interpreter ... to instruct them to submit. Pak So persevered and did not surrender. The Mongols then built scaling ladders and assaulted the city. Pak So met and attacked them with large slashing implements. There were none that were not smashed and the ladders could not approach. During the siege an old Mongol general of seventy years of age toured beneath the city walls to look over the city ramparts and equipment. He sighed and said, 'I have followed the army since I bound my hair into plaits as a youth and so I am accustomed to seeing the cities of the earth attacked and fought over. Still, I have never seen a city undergo an attack like this that did not in the end submit.'

While Kuju was still holding out, three Korean armies left Kaesong to march north to its relief, but while Yi Chasong, the leader of the vanguard, was resting his men, a surprise attack by 8,000 Mongols came upon them. An arrow hit Yi, and a spear felled his companion. With the relieving force thus thrown into disarray the Mongols redoubled their efforts against Kuju, but as it still refused to surrender

they detached an army for a raid to the south, taking P'yongju, while other Mongol raids spread as far south as Ch'ungju and Ch'ongju. This brought their armies very close to Kaesong, so the terrified Koryo government opened negotiations with the invaders.

Unfortunately for the brave defenders of Kuju, the Koryo government at Kaesong succeeded in negotiating its surrender behind their backs. Pak So was astounded and refused to surrender following an order from the king. He received a sentence of execution, and it was only the intervention from his admiring Mongol enemies that saved him. The new tribute demanded from Korea by the Mongols was enormous. It included gold, silver, pearls, 10,000 otter skins, 20,000 horses, 10,000 bolts of silk and clothing for one million soldiers. In addition, thousands of hostages were to be handed over, and Mongol officers were to be stationed in the principle Korean cities. Korea appeared to be doomed, but a strange development lay just ahead.

In 1232 the Korean court slipped away from Kaesong and took refuge on the fortified island of Kanghwa. This was the first time in any campaign the Mongols had been faced with a sea barrier. The water, though only half a mile (1km) wide, saved the island from being captured. (Author's collection)

The stubborn resistance of Kuju had been a further illustration of the difficulties posed to the Mongols by operations against fortified cities. In spite of Chinese bombs and Korean ingenuity these challenges were being steadily overcome, but the Korean campaign was soon to reveal a further weakness in Mongol warfare. In 1232 the Koryo court slipped away from Kaesong and took refuge on the fortified island of Kanghwa. For the first time in any campaign the Mongols were faced with a sea barrier. In spite of all attempts to overcome Kanghwa they did not succeed in capturing the island, even though the watery gap was only half a mile (1km) wide.

Frustrated by the insult posed by Kanghwa, the Mongols took to their more familiar roles of raiding and devastation elsewhere as a way of forcing the Korean king to submit. In August 1232 Sartaq swept southwards into the Han river valley south of present-day Seoul and besieged a small mountain fortress called Ch'oin. It was defended vigorously under the command of a warrior monk called Kim Yunhu. A Korean monk archer, possibly Kim himself, succeeded in placing an arrow into Sartaq's eye. With their commander dead the Mongols raised the siege and left Korea. The second invasion had come to an abrupt end.

The third Mongol invasion of Korea

Korea was among the targets listed at the epic *kuriltai* held by the Mongol high command in 1235 that also launched the invasion of Europe and the campaign against the Southern Song. In acknowledgement of the fierce resistance previously mounted

against them, the best Mongol troops were assigned to the Korean theatre, and it is interesting to note that the only other area of operation for which crack troops were earmarked was mighty Russia.

The third Mongol progress down the Korean peninsula was facilitated by the defection to the Mongol camp of a Koryo official who treacherously handed P'yongyang over to the invaders. With their rear safeguarded, and ignoring the Korean court in its fastness of Kanghwa, the armies continued southwards as far as Kyongju, and the action fought en route at Ch'ukju produced another epic of siege warfare. Unlike the walled city of Kuju, Ch'ukju was a *sansong* (mountain castle) with low walls of stone and earth encircling a natural amphitheatre. Refusing a Mongol

Another siege took place at Ch'ungju in 1253, where the Korean commander was the warrior monk, Kim Yunhu, of Ch'oin fame. He ensured the support of all the population by publicly burning the slave registers, and would not surrender. But at nearby Ch'ungju the Mongols created a total blockade of the town so that its inhabitants were reduced to drinking the blood of their livestock. When Ch'ungju fell, everyone in it was slaughtered.

At about this time another initiative began that had as its aim the expulsion of the Mongols through religious activity. During one of the earlier Khitan incursions in the year 1011 a set of wooden printing blocks for the canon of the Buddhist scriptures had been laboriously carved as a votive offering for expelling the invaders. It was piously believed to have been successful, but this set of blocks had been destroyed by fire during the Mongol invasion of 1231. The task was therefore begun again as a way of imploring divine help for salvation from the new terror of the Mongols.

The carving was begun in 1237 at the Chondungsa temple on Kanghwa Island and was completed in 1251. It is amazing to note that, in spite of all the warfare that has raged across the Korean peninsula since that date, the blocks, known as the *Tripitaka Koreana*, are still in existence. They consist of 81,340 printing blocks, and may be seen today at the Haiensa temple, where a simple but effective natural air-conditioning system has kept them in perfect condition for seven centuries. To the Koreans this long-lasting and pious endeavour was fully justified in 1254 when the Mongols withdrew their armies. Ch'ungju remained untaken, and a further amphibious operation against Kanghwa Island had proved to be a disaster. The votive offering had triumphed, but would the Mongols return?

warning to surrender, the commander, Song Munju, hit back using catapults and drove the besiegers from the walls. Once again the Mongols resorted to the tactic of using catapult-projected incendiaries based on bales of straw soaked in human fat, but General Song withstood all their assaults, and earned himself a reputation that was to rank alongside Pak So at Kuju.

OPPOSITE By withstanding all the Mongol assaults,
General Song Munju earned himself a famous reputation.
(Author's collection)

BELOW The *Inpitaka Kureana* printing blocks may be seen
today at the Haiensa temple, where they have been kept in
perfect condition for seven centuries. (Author's collection)

The final Mongol invasion of Korea

Only a few months passed before the Koreans' worst fears were realised when the Mongol army invaded Korea in 1254 for what was to prove the last time. Korean resistance was immediate and as determined as ever. Ch'ungju was attacked again, but its defenders were helped by a fortuitous storm that forced a quick Mongol withdrawal, and p'yolch'o activity was even more extensive than before. Kanghwa still remained inviolate, so the Mongols began to construct fortifications of their own in Korea from which they could launch widespread raids with some security. This included a wall round their border possession of Uiju.

The new Mongol strategy proved to be a decisive shift in the fortunes of war and in 1258 radical developments within Korean politics also greatly helped the Mongol cause. Throughout all the previous invasions the resistance from Kanghwa had been controlled not by the Korean king but by the hard-line anti-Mongol Ch'oe family, who were virtually Korea's military dictators. When the incumbent ruler, Ch'oe Ui, was assassinated in 1258, King Kojong assumed personal control of the government and indicated his intention to negotiate a peace. Hostages were sent to the Mongol court as proof of good intentions, but a group of die-hard Korean military officers deposed the new king, Wongjong, and determined to keep fighting. Their success was a brief one, because Mongol troops were invited in by the Korean royal family to overthrow the rebels, which they did in 1270, the insurgents fleeing to Cheju Island. In 1273, in a final diplomatic settlement, the Korean crown prince was married to Khubilai Khan's daughter, and with this alliance the resistance from Cheju ceased.

Half of Cheju Island was given over to a grazing ground for Mongol horses in a process of pacification that was paralleled throughout mainland Korea. At first the Mongols appeared to be generous overlords, and it seemed that peace had finally come to the peninsula. But only one year would pass before the Korean king was humiliated when his country's soldiers and naval resources were commandeered by the Mongols for their most ambitious maritime project of all: the invasion of Japan.

The Russian and European theatre 1237–42

As noted above, following the kuriltai of 1235 the finest Mongol troops were allocated for the operations against Korea and Russia, and in both cases this had come about because of an acute appreciation by the Mongols of the nature of the tasks that lay ahead. Korea was a small country bitterly defended, while Russia was an enormous land where resistance was also likely to be very fierce, because, as in the Korean case, the Mongols had already had a taste of what was to come from the battle of the Kalka river, described below. This encounter provided the Mongols with vital intelligence about their foes, but on the opposing side the mood was of utter confusion, because as far as the Russians could tell, the invaders then simply disappeared. 'They turned back from the river Dnieper, and we know not whence they came and whither they went,' wrote the Novgorodian chronicler. 'Only God knows that, because he brought them upon us for our sins.' In fact, 14 years would pass before these mysterious invaders returned.

The northern campaign

The Mongols' reappearance in Russian lands should have come as no surprise to their victims, because during the intervening years certain neighbouring peoples were attacked as a means of safeguarding future Mongol communications. Thus it was that in 1229 Saksin and Bulgar-on-the-Volga were overrun, as were the Polovtsians who then 'fled to the Bulgars' for refuge. The Bulgars themselves were attacked again in 1232, and even when a further Bulgar campaign released a flood of refugees into Russian lands, the princes failed to take any extraordinary defence measures or to properly co-ordinate their military plans.

The subsequent Mongol invasion of Russia between 1237 and 1240 was devastating in its execution and long-lasting in its effects. The experience in Poland and Hungary, which took place as part of the overall European operation, ended with the Mongols withdrawing after the campaigns, but the Russian wars resulted in the 'Tartar yoke' that was to control Russia under the Golden Horde for longer than the Yuan dynasty ruled China.

The great Mongol invasion of Russia may be divided into two phases. The first was the invasion of north-east Russia between December 1237 and the spring of 1238, and the second was the invasion of south-western Russia and Ukraine between 1239 and 1240. The decision to begin with a northern campaign was in all probability due to Subadai's assessment that one reason for the Mongol success at the battle of the Kalka river had been the inactivity of Grand Duke Vladimir of Vladimir/Suzdal. Choosing winter in which to launch the campaign was also a product of Subadai's military skills. Unlike Napoleon and Hitler, whose invasions of the Russian lands famously ended with the intervention of 'Generals January and February', Subadai commanded an army that found frozen lands and rivers much to their liking for speeding their progress across the vast steppes.

The Mongols' first objective in the northern campaign against Vladimir/Suzdal was the city of Riazan on the Oka river. The southern half of the principality was neutralised when Belgorod and Pronsk to the south-west of Riazan were taken, and then the city itself was targeted in a siege that began on 16 December 1237 and was over by 21 December. The Mongols approached the city and:

... surrounded it with a palisade; the prince of Riazan shut himself in the town with his people. The Tartars took the town of Riazan on the twenty-first of the same month, and burned it all, and killed its prince Yuri and his princess and seized the men, women and children, the monks, nuns and priests; some they struck down with swords, while others they shot with arrows and flung into the flames; still others they seized and bound, cut and disembowelled their bodies.

This description of the horrors from the *Voskresensk Chronicle* is echoed by a longer account entitled *The Tale of the Destruction of Riazan*:

Batu changed his regiments frequently, replacing them with fresh troops, while the citizens of Riazan fought without relief ... On the dawn of the sixth day the pagan warriors began to storm the city, some with firebrands, some with battering rams, and others with countless scaling ladders for ascending the walls of the city.

A similar description of the slaughter in the city and the drowning of captives in the river follows, then:

... they burned this holy city with all its beauty and wealth, and they captured the relatives of the Riazan princes, the princes of Kiev and Chernigov. And churches of God

The Mongols approached the Golden Gate of Vladimir and showed to the defenders Prince Vladimir, one of Yuri's sons whom they had captured. (Author's collection)

The Mongol invasion of Europe, 1237–1242

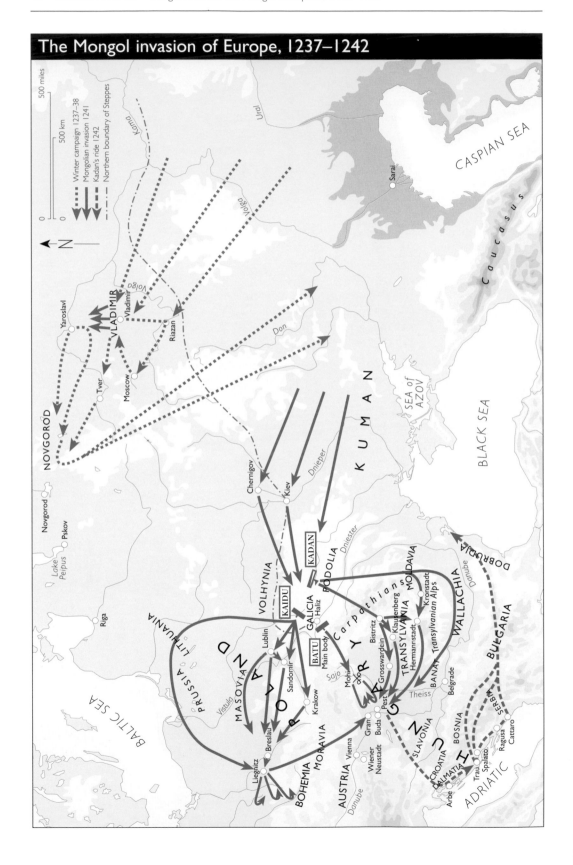

Legend:
- Winter campaign 1237–38
- Mongolian invasion 1241
- Kadan's ride 1242
- Northern boundary of Steppes

500 miles
500 km

←N—

CASPIAN SEA

Sarai

Caucasus

BLACK SEA

SEA of AZOV

KUMAN

Don

Dnieper

Dniester

Volga

Kama

Ural

NOVGOROD
Yaroslavl
VLADIMIR
Vladimir
Tver
Moscow
Riazan

Novgorod
Pskov
Lake Peipus

Chernigov
Kiev

KADAN
PODOLIA

KAIDU
VOLHYNIA
GALICIA
Haliz

BATU
Main body

Riga

LITHUANIA
PRUSSIA
BALTIC SEA

Lublin
Sandomir
Krakow
Breslau
Liegnitz

MASOVIA
POLAND
BOHEMIA
MORAVIA

Vistula

AUSTRIA
Vienna
Wiener Neustadt
Danube

Gran
Buda
Pest
Mohi
Sajo
Grosswardein
HUNGARY

Theiss

Carpathians
Bistritz
Klausenberg
Hermannstadt
TRANSYLVANIA
Kronstadt
Transylvanian Alps
MOLDAVIA

BANAT

Belgrade
SERBIA
Belgrade
SLAVONIA
CROATIA
BOSNIA
DALMATIA
Arbe
Trau
Spalato
Ragusa
Cattaro
ADRIATIC

WALLACHIA
Danube
DOBRUDJA
BULGARIA

were destroyed, and much blood was spilled on the holy altars. And not one man was left alive in the city. All were dead. All had drunk the same bitter cup to the dregs, and there was not anyone to mourn the dead. Neither father nor mother could mourn their dead children ...

A relief force sent by Grand Duke Yuri II arrived too late, and then the Mongols defeated another relief force from Suzdal

After Riazan, the Mongols captured and burned Moscow, then just a minor fortified outpost. (Author's collection)

near the town of Kolomna. Moving on from Riazan the Mongols took and burned the then minor fortified outpost called Moscow. The capital, Vladimir, was now outflanked, so Grand Duke Yuri decided to retreat northwards to organise resistance from above the Upper Volga river. He obviously had great faith in the fortifications of Vladimir, because he left his wife and two of his sons there. The Mongol forces also divided, following his every move. Part of their army proceeded to nearby Suzdal, which they easily captured, then rejoined the main force for an attack on Vladimir. Meanwhile the Mongol vanguard headed northwards to monitor Yuri's own army where it had assembled on the banks of the Sit river.

The *Voskresensk Chronicle* tells us how the Mongols approached the Golden Gate of Vladimir and showed to the defenders Prince Vladimir, one of Yuri's sons, whom they had captured. To this psychological ploy was soon added the spectacle of seeing hundreds of other Russian prisoners being forced to build a palisade around the beleaguered city. Then the attack began:

On Sunday February 8 early in the morning the Tartars approached the city from all sides and began to hit the city with rams, and began to pour great stones into the centre of the city from far away, as if by God's will, as if it rained inside the city; many people were killed inside the city and all were greatly frightened and trembled.

When the bombardment was judged to have done sufficient damage the Mongols 'entered like demons', killing Yuri's sons among countless other people. When the news reached Prince Yuri that his capital had been destroyed, he bravely prepared to face the victorious Mongol army from his position on the Sit river. 'Prince Yuri forgot about fear and advanced to meet them,' says the *Voskresensk Chronicle*. 'Regiments met and there ensued a major battle and fierce slaughter; blood flowed like water.' But the Russian army was defeated and Grand Duke Yuri II was slain.

While this battle was being fought, another Mongol detachment headed off and captured Tver and Torzhok. The road to Novgorod the Great, the major trading centre of European Russia, was now wide open but spring was fast approaching and, with it, the prospect of seas of mud that would hinder the Mongol advance. According to the *Chronicle of Novgorod*, 'the great and sacred apostolic cathedral Church of Santa Sophia protected Novgorod' so the Mongols withdrew. They did not head back the way they had come – where all supplies had been destroyed – but instead moved through the untouched lands to the south, avoiding almost all fortified places. The one exception was the town of Kozelsk, which refused to surrender and held out for seven weeks. The Mongol army then set up camp and rested in the Don basin. The first phase of the invasion was over.

The southern campaign

In 1239, refreshed and re-equipped, Batu's armies were ready to resume their advance against Russia, but only comparatively minor military operations were undertaken that year. These included the final submission of the Polovtsians. Many Polovtsians preferred to migrate to Hungary under Khan Kotyan, and their arrival there would later provide an excuse for the Mongol campaign against Hungary. The other important inroads were successes that paved the way for a 'southern campaign' against Russia to begin in earnest in 1240. First Pereyaslavl fell, then Chernigov (Chernihiv), and the next target was the ancient city of Kiev (Kyiv). A governor appointed by Prince Daniel of Galicia ruled Kiev. When Mongol envoys arrived he ordered their execution to stiffen the resolve of the inhabitants, and soon afterwards Mongol soldiers were at the gates:

The Tartar force besieged it and it was impossible for anyone either to leave the city or to enter it. Squeaking of wagons, bellowing of camels, sounds of trumpets and organs, neighing of horses, and cries and sobs of an innumerable multitude of people made it impossible to hear one another in the city.

The walls were soon breached as effectively as at Riazan and Vladimir, and a day and night of fierce fighting followed across the rubble. Then a familiar pattern of slaughter began in the streets:

During the night the inhabitants built a new fortification around the Church of the Virgin Mary [the Church of the Tithe]. When morning came the Tartars attacked them and there was a bitter slaughter. Some people fainted and some fled to the church roof with their possessions; and the church walls collapsed from the weight and the Tartars took the city of Kiev.

Six years later Giovanni de Piano Carpini, the Pope's envoy to the Mongol Khan, passed through Kiev on his way to the east, and wrote:

When we were journeying through that land we came across countless skulls and bones of dead men lying about on the ground. Kiev had been a very large and thickly populated town, but now it has been reduced almost to nothing, for there are at the present time scarcely two hundred houses there and the inhabitants are kept in complete slavery.

The Polish campaign

The Mongols' southern campaign continued with a Polish campaign and a major advance against Hungary, where the defeated Polovtsians had fled, although their destruction was by no means the primary motivation for the Mongol incursion. The main consideration was a strategic one, because they believed that the flat grasslands of Hungary would make an ideal grazing ground to act as a forward base for any future advance into western Europe.

While Batu, accompanied by Subadai, forced the Carpathians he sent Baidar and Kaidu, the sons of Jagatai, to make a diversion against Poland and sent Kadan into Transylvania. The former action turned out to be much more than a reconnaissance raid and resulted in quite a major campaign. It also provided the Mongols with one of their most celebrated victories at the battle of Leignitz.

The Polish operation began with a very profitable raid. The Mongols ravaged as far as the Vistula (Wisla) river, burning towns such as Lublin. They then crossed the Vistula on the ice on 13 February 1241, and burned and sacked Sandomir (Sandomiercz), after which some brave knights of Malopolska (Lesser Poland) met them in battle at Cmielnik to the north-west of Krakow. They perished to a man in a battle on 18 March that is totally overshadowed in historical memory by the famous battle of Leignitz that was to come soon afterwards.

Having advanced to within a few miles of Krakow the Mongols began to withdraw with their booty, satisfied at the initial outcome of

One of the secrets to Mongol mobility was the *ger*, popularly known as the *yurt*, shown here in a modern Mongol encampment. (David Sneath)

Henry the Pious, Duke of Silesia, sets out to meet the Mongols in battle. (Author's collection)

their endeavours, but so alarming had been this irruption into Poland that Boleslaw the Chaste, prince of Krakow, fled for his life, and so many followed him that the Mongols were able to enter Krakow virtually unopposed. There was therefore no siege of Krakow comparable to the siege of Kiev, but the destruction meted out to the abandoned city was very similar.

The Mongol army then continued westwards where the next important city was Breslau (Wroclaw), the capital of Silesia. Crossing the river Oder at Ratibor, some on rafts and some swimming, the Mongols approached Breslau ready for a siege, but found that its inhabitants had done their work for them, burning the town themselves and taking refuge in the citadel.

Here the Mongol main body was rejoined by a detachment under Kaidu that had taken a more northerly route, and scouts informed them that a hostile army had taken up a position against them not far to the west of Breslau at Wahlstatt near Leignitz. A decision now had to be made over whether to attack the castle of Breslau first or to take on the Polish army, which was under the command of Henry the Pious, Duke of Silesia. Czech and German knights were also present, and a persistent tradition claims that a contingent of Teutonic Knights was also there, possibly under their Grand Master Poppo of Osterna, although this has been called into question.

As Henry marched out from Leignitz with his army a stone fell from a church and nearly struck him. This was inevitably taken as a bad omen, and it was therefore with some trepidation that he arranged his forces into four divisions on the fateful battlefield. The Mongols left Breslau and advanced to fight him, and appear to have adopted their favourite tactic of a false withdrawal to lure their enemies on. The allied army seems to have been initially thrown into confusion volleys of Mongol arrows, but rallied sufficiently to mount a charge against the Mongols, at which the Mongols carefully withdrew.

At this point great alarm was caused in the allied ranks by a man who appeared out of the Mongol ranks on horseback and

The battle of Leignitz as depicted on the ceiling of the church at Legmia Pole, the site of the battle. Note at the right the smokescreen appearing out of the Mongol standard. (Author's collection)

galloped around crying out in Polish, 'Fly, fly!' This apparition no doubt accompanied the Mongol counter-attack. Some of the army retreated, but Henry the Pious charged the Mongols once again. The chronicler Dluglosz (who is also the main source for the Polish victory at Grunwald/Tannenberg in 1410 and therefore not a contemporary eye-witness) includes a vivid description of the Mongol *tuk* (standard) made from crossed bones and yak tails, which he describes as being 'a Greek cross, on top of which was a grey head with a beard'. He also mentions the strange phenomenon of clouds of burning foul-smelling smoke that the Mongols used at Leignitz. It was probably produced by burning reeds, fanned by a favourable wind. With this acting as both an irritant and a smoke screen the Mongols pressed home their advantage. Duke Henry escaped with four of his followers. Three were killed, and then the duke's own horse gave way. After a brave combat he was slain and his head was cut off.

The body of Henry the Pious was identified later by his wife only because of the six toes he had on one foot. He was the most distinguished out of hundreds of victims who fell at Leignitz on 9 April, because we are told that the Mongols filled nine sacks with the ears cut off from the slain. Henry's head was impaled upon a spear and paraded outside the walls of his castle at Leignitz. The defenders were suitably terrified, but Leignitz was not a major Mongol target, so the Mongols abandoned Poland and marched on into Bohemia and Moravia, heading in the general direction of their main objective of Hungary. No major battles are recorded for Moravia, but we can have some inkling of the devastation that must have occurred from the records of towns that later received economic help, such as the granting of free markets, to assist them in their recovery after the invaders had passed through.

The Hungarian campaign

While the Polish campaign had been turning Hungary's northern flank, Kadan's lesser-

known operation had entered through Moldavia and Wallachia to the east and south. Transylvania was ravaged as the armies passed through, with most damage being done to the city of Varadin, which suffered a fate akin to that of Kiev and Vladimir. This Mongol army then rejoined Batu and Subadai's central column to rendezvous on the eastern bank of the Danube between 2 and 5 April.

The mighty Danube river had the potential to act as a powerful natural barrier against the Mongols. It was, after all, much wider than the sea barrier at Kanghwa in Korea. It was therefore unfortunate for the Hungarians that their rulers were incapable of putting up a united front that would match the challenge of their great river. King Bela IV faced opposition from rival barons, and had also caused resentment by accepting into Hungary the fleeing Polovtsians, who had responded to the Hungarians' granting of asylum by raiding and plundering. To make matters worse, while the Mongols were already marching across Hungary, rumours spread that the Polovtsians had invited the

At the battle of Leignitz Henry lies dead beneath horses' hooves. (Author's collection)

King Bela IV of Hungary, from his statue at Visegrad. (Author's collection)

Mongols to join them in Hungary, and even that they and the Mongols were one and the same race. Riots began, and the Polovtsians hit back, so Hungary suffered raids from two sources. In one incident the bishop of Varadin was defeated by a classic Mongol false retreat when he went in pursuit of them after they had raided Erlau (Eger). It was near Eger that the great disaster of the battle of Mohi (on the Sajo river) came upon the Hungarian army.

King Bela escaped from Mohi, as did his brother, Coloman, who made it to his territories of Croatia and Dalmatia, only to die there of his wounds. When King Bela reached Pressburg (Bratislava) in safety to take refuge with Duke Frederick of Austria, the latter was contemptuous of the Hungarians' plight and extracted a large ransom from the king before sending him on his way to Croatia.

With the government of Hungary shattered, the Mongol armies advanced triumphantly to Pest, but in front of them lay the great expanse of the Danube. Buda was at that time only a minor settlement compared with mighty Gran (Esztergom) so the Mongols did not cross there but followed the outside curve of the Danube bend to reach the shore of modern Slovakia opposite Gran late in December. The river had frozen over, providing an ideal way of crossing, so Gran was fiercely attacked. Its defenders fought back bravely from the citadel overlooking the Danube where the cathedral now stands. The Mongols bombarded Gran's wooden fortifications with 30 catapults to make a breach, and filled in the ditch using sacks of earth. When the city was entered on Christmas Day 1241 the inhabitants set fire to their own homes and buried their valuables so that the Mongols would not have them. Many people were roasted over slow fires to make them disclose where they had hidden their treasures.

Meanwhile a separate Mongol army under Kadan had been detached and sent in search of King Bela. This unit crossed the Danube between Pest and Buda and marched on to the old Hungarian capital of Stûhlweissenburg (Szekesfehervar). They burned the outskirts but the town was saved when a sudden thaw of the frozen ground caused flooding. The Mongol way now led via Lake Balaton to a crossing of the Drava river into Croatia. The Mongols soon captured Zagreb, and before very long they were in sight of the Adriatic at Spalatro.

At this point Kadan seems to have been confronted by a repetition of the Kanghwa situation when King Bela took ship and sailed along the coast to Trau. When the Mongols prepared to attack Trau, Bela returned to his ship and anchored offshore. So the Mongols instead continued their raids into Bosnia, passing through Ragusa (Dubrovnik) and on into Albania, reaching almost as far as Scutari when Kadan was recalled by Batu. This was the most southerly point reached in the whole of the European operation. A separate Mongol campaign arising out of the devastation of Hungary followed the southern bend of the Danube past Bratislava on the opposite bank and advanced as far as Wiener Neustadt, where an army under Duke Frederick caused them to retire.

The battle of Mohi (Sajo river), 1241

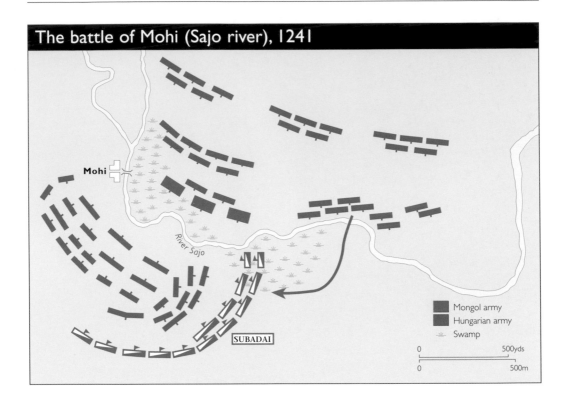

Mohi

River Sajo

SUBADAI

Mongol army
Hungarian army
Swamp

0   500yds
0   500m

The view of the Danube at Gran (Esztergom), captured by the Mongols during the Hungarian campaign. (Author's collection)

A view of Margaret Island on the Danube in Budapest and the Pest shore looking from Buda castle. (Author's collection)

The Mongol yoke

Although no one would have guessed it at the time, the Mongols had withdrawn from central Europe never to return. In September 1242 word reached Batu that Ogedei Khan had died on 11 December 1241 either from excessive drinking or possibly by poison. Batu's presence was needed at a *kuriltai* to elect a successor. So instead of wintering in Hungary ready for another attack the Mongol armies melted away.

As the situation in western Europe at that time was one of such divisions it is tempting to speculate what the results might have been if the Mongols had not disappeared. The main area of rivalry lay between the Pope and the Holy Roman Emperor, each of whom called for crusades against the Mongols while accusing his rival of supporting the invaders. The result of the fragmentation of effort had been that King Bela IV received no help when he so desperately needed it, and the only

contemporary movement that called itself a crusade had nothing to do with fighting the Mongols at all. This was the march against Novgorod by the army of the Teutonic Knights of Livonia, which ensured that two enemies threatened this important Russian town. The campaign ended with the defeat of the crusaders by Alexander Nevsky in the famous 'battle on the ice' at Lake Peipus.

So the Mongols withdrew from Hungary, and when it was considered safe enough King Bela IV returned to see for himself the devastation that the invaders had caused, but in spite of all the folklore about the Mongols disappearing, that was certainly not the impression given to the inhabitants of the lands that had been the Mongols' first target in this long-lasting campaign. Batu's withdrawing armies established themselves in the Russian steppes north of the Black Sea and the Caspian Sea. At Sarai on the lower Volga, Batu set up the capital of the Golden Horde, who proceeded to rule and to extract tribute from a huge steppe territory from the Danube in the west to Khwarazm in the east. The southern end included the Crimean peninsula and the

North Caucasus, while in the north it took in the conquered lands of the Russians.

The princes of these lands who had survived or succeeded to vacant thrones following the burnings at Vladimir and Kiev now set themselves to the tasks of rebuilding their cities and establishing a working relationship with the conquerors. The Mongols wished to rule through local dignitaries, so in 1243, for example, Prince Iaroslav Vsevolodich, who had replaced his brother Yuri as prince of Vladimir after the latter's death at the battle of the Sit river, made a 'trip to the Horde' as the chronicler terms it. He was awarded the title of Grand Prince of Vladimir and also Grand Prince of Kiev. Prince Mikhail of Chernigov had a less pleasant experience when he visited Sarai. He was ordered to purify himself by walking between two fires and then told to bow before an idol of Genghis Khan. When he refused he was executed, and was recognised later as a saint of the Russian Orthodox Church. The 'Mongol yoke' of the Golden Horde had been firmly laid across Russian shoulders.

King Bela sees for himself the devastation caused in Hungary by the Mongols. (Author's collection)

The Middle-Eastern theatre 1251–60

By comparison with the European campaigns of 1237–1242 the Mongol progress in the Islamic world had been slow but steady, but an important development occurred in 1251 when Hulegu was sent on a military campaign into south-west Asia by his brother Mongke, the newly elected Khan. His overall brief was to subject 'the Western countries and the various lands of the Sultan'.

The destruction of the Assassins

Hulegu left Mongolia in 1253 and took three years to complete the long journey towards his first objective, which was the headquarters of the Ismailis, a heretical sect of Islam otherwise known as the Assassins from their use of the drug hashish. Their use of murder as a political and religious weapon has meant that the word 'assassin' has entered our language in a very different context. This was a particularly challenging operation for the Mongols, because the Assassins were based in a series of castles located on the tops of hills within dry valleys near the Caspian Sea in Iran.

Hulegu defeated the Assassins of Persia, and then went on to capture Baghdad in a fine military career that followed the Mongol tradition of conquest. (Author's collection)

The Mongols used large Chinese-style siege crossbows against them, positioning them on mountain peaks opposite the fortresses to give a horizontal trajectory. The siege crossbow is described by Juvaini as an 'ox's bow which had been constructed by Khitan craftsmen and had a range of 2,500 paces'. Teams of 'athletes' were stationed about 300 yards apart to transport the frames and poles of the collapsible crossbows up the slopes. Hulegu himself commanded from one of these vantage points:

Arrows, which were the shaft of Doom discharged by the Angel of Death, were let fly against these wretches, passing like hail through the sieve-like clouds.

The Assassins used traction trebuchets and hand-held crossbows against any Mongol attackers climbing up on foot. The Mongols also used large fire arrows loosed from their siege crossbows. This won them more ground, and during peace negotiations the Mongols took advantage of the coming and going of the messengers to find more suitable sites for their catapults and to assemble them undisturbed. The next day a general assault began from these new and greatly advantageous positions. The use of the word 'mangonels' in the accounts suggest that traction trebuchets had now been added to the Mongol armoury. The Ismailis took what shelter they could from the dual bombardment, but after some fierce fighting the castles surrendered.

The conquest of Syria

By 1256 Hulegu had completed the first phase of his campaign and could turn his attentions to further Islamic conquests. Most of the rulers of Iran had already made their submission to the Mongols, but one outstanding figure who had not bent the knee was the Caliph of Baghdad. The Caliph may have exercised little real authority beyond that city, but his religious and political influence in the Islamic world was tremendous, and it must have annoyed the Mongols to hear of him proclaiming the same sort of nominal universal sovereignty that the Mongol Khan claimed for himself.

A Mongol army laid siege to Baghdad in 1258 and intimidated the inhabitants by sending arrow letters over the walls, stating that only non-combatants and certain high officials would be spared. We are told that the Mongols were short of catapult projectiles and had to make do with sections cut from palm trees or with stones brought from three or four days' journey away, but these sufficed to assist in the capture of the eastern wall. Some people tried to escape down the river, but were driven back by a hail of stones and naphtha bombs. When the city was taken the Caliph was put to death.

Even before Baghdad was captured there is evidence that Hulegu already had the idea of pushing on to Syria and Egypt, where they would come into contact with another legendary band of fierce mounted warriors in

The Ismailis, a heretical sect of Islam, otherwise known as the Assassins, provided a challenge for the Mongols. The Assassins were based in castles located on the tops of hills within dry valleys near the Caspian Sea in Iran. This photograph shows the castle of Samiran. (David Nicolle)

the form of the Mamluks. The Mamluks were slave soldiers, mostly of Turkish origin, who had been taken from their homes and converted to Islam. They underwent strict military training and fought as mounted archers for their patrons, to whom they maintained a fierce loyalty. Some of these Mamluks owed their origins to earlier Mongol campaigns, and in fact slaves taken from the defeated Polovtsians are believed to have ended up fighting against the Mongols in Syria in 1260.

The Mongol invasion of Syria began with the customary exploratory raid, and then, on 18 December 1259, a Mongol army under Hulegu, together with Georgian, Armenian and Seljuk Rum (Anatolian) troops, crossed the Euphrates and took up positions outside Aleppo. The siege lasted a week, and was followed by the usual slaughter and looting, although Aleppo's famous citadel held out for a further month. When it eventually fell the building was demolished but, unusually, the defenders were allowed to live. After this success Hulegu marched westwards and took Harim, then returned to Aleppo where he received delegations of dignitaries from Hama and Homs who had come to surrender their cities.

The citadel of Aleppo. (Thom Richardson)

Up to this point the campaign had been a straightforward one. Even before the fall of Aleppo, Hulegu had sent an army under his trusted general Ketbugha on exploratory expeditions to the south. Ketbugha was placed in charge of Syria at Damascus when Hulegu withdrew in 1260, supposedly in response to the news of the death of his brother Mongke Khan. This had led to a succession dispute between his other brothers, Arige-boke and Khubilai. The result was that Syria was left under Mongol control, but only a small army of 10,000 men defended it. Nevertheless, Ketbugha continued to act with the customary Mongol self-confidence, sending a raiding party into Palestine as far as Gaza. Hebron, Jerusalem and Nablus are recorded as being among the other targets. The force was safely back in Damascus by the spring of 1260.

The battle of Ain Jalut

As events were shortly to prove, the real challenge to Mongol supremacy in the Middle East lay not in Syria but in Egypt, where a former Mamluk slave called Qutuz had seized power and become Sultan in 1259. From the beginning of his reign Qutuz pursued a vigorous anti-Mongol policy. The Mongol threat had conveniently provided the pretext for his coup, and the perceived danger was strengthened when Hulegu sent Qutuz a letter calling on him to submit. The missive disparaged Qutuz's lowly slave origins as, 'He is of the race of Mamluks who fled before our sword into this country, who enjoyed its comforts and then killed its rulers.' When Qutuz ordered the execution of the Mongol envoys, as so many other rulers in a similar position had done, war became inevitable.

Qutuz was determined not to wait for a Mongol invasion of Egypt but to march into Palestine himself. He was aware that the Mongol army left behind under Ketbugha was a comparatively small one, and his advance was an attempt to seize the initiative. The Mamluk vanguard under Baybars moved forward to collect information about the Mongols, and encountered them first in the shape of an advance guard near Gaza, whom they forced to flee. Qutuz followed them and moved up the coast to Acre, which was then held by a crusader army. The crusaders were enthralled by the prospect of a battle between Mongols and a Muslim army, and chose to remain neutral, although they sent supplies to Qutuz in acknowledgement of the recent sacking of Sidon by the Mongols.

Ketbugha was in the Biqa valley when he received the news that the Mamluks had entered Syria, so he gathered his troops who were then widely scattered on garrison duties or grazing and headed south. He took up a position at Ain Jalut ('Goliath's spring') north-west of Mount Gilboa. It was an excellent place for a cavalry battle, and the adjacent valley offered good pasture. Baybar's Mamluk vanguard made contact with the Mongols through some extensive skirmishing, and on ascending a hill observed the Mongol positions. The Mongols had also noted him, so he beat a hasty retreat to join Qutuz and the main body.

The battle of Ain Jalut took place on Friday 3 September 1260. The Mamluks approached from the north-west, and the Mongols charged into them, destroying the Mamluk left flank. But Qutuz rallied his troops and launched a counter-attack that shook the Mongols. They again attacked, but Qutuz again rallied his men to the cry of 'Allah – help your servant Qutuz against the Mongols!' He then launched a frontal attack that led to a complete Mamluk victory. Ketbugha was killed, and the Mongol army disintegrated. There followed a pursuit of the Mongol stragglers, and the Mongols received a taste of their own medicine for the first time.

Ain Jalut had therefore provided that rarest of events, a Mongol defeat, and it is thus often regarded as being a turning point in the Mongol conquests. Islam had been saved, the Mongols had been stopped and the myth of their invincibility had been destroyed. In fact all the above assertions are somewhat exaggerated, because the Mongol army destroyed at Ain Jalut was only a small part of the total force available to them. One day they would return.

Part of the ancient fortifications of the city of Damascus, which were abandoned as the Mongols approached. (Thom Richardson)

Nevertheless, 21 years were to pass before another Mongol army came to Syria, a breathing space similar to that enjoyed by other nations at other times. The difference was that this breathing space had been bought not by the need for a Mongol commander to return to elect a new Khan, but by a genuine military defeat for which the Mamluks and their leaders deserve every credit. Since the time of the unification of the Mongol tribes, Genghis Khan and his descendants had spent little time fighting their own kind. The Mamluks were horse archers like themselves whose origins lay in the Eurasian steppes. As one historian put it, 'the infidels of yesterday had defeated the Muslims of tomorrow'.

The southern Chinese theatre 1254–79

The Mongols pressed forward their conquest of the Southern Song from 1254 onwards in a huge operation hindered temporarily by the death of Mongke Khan in 1259. The effort was resumed by Khubilai and was a colossal military undertaking that faced numerous obstacles. The Mongol armies were not used to the climate or the terrain of the south and were also faced with some formidable walled towns, so the final assault on the Southern Song was based on a strategy of a grand detour. First, a southwards drive cutting across Sichuan and Yunnan went as far as the Vietnamese border. Second, the city of Xiangyang was targeted, so that the Mongols could follow the Yangtze downstream.

The southern Chinese operation by Khubilai paralleled that of his brother, Hulegu, in the Islamic world, and in 1253 the first half of the bid to outflank the Southern Song succeeded when Khubilai destroyed the Nanzhao kingdom based at its capital of Dali in Yunnan. Uriyangkhadai, the son of the famous Subadai, conducted

the operation. Direct action against the Song, however, had to wait a few years, and hostilities actually commenced with raids on the Mongols by the Song between 1260 and 1262. Early in 1265 the first major battle erupted. The two armies clashed at Diaoyu in Sichuan province, and the Mongols not only won the battle but captured 146 ships. The confiscation of the vessels showed that Khubilai Khan appreciated that the Mongols now needed a navy, and the speed with which this was set in motion impressed a Chinese historian who wrote, 'the alacrity with which the Mongols, a nation of horsemen unacquainted with the sea, took to naval warfare was amazing'.

Khubilai Khan, the first Yuan emperor of China. (Author's collection)

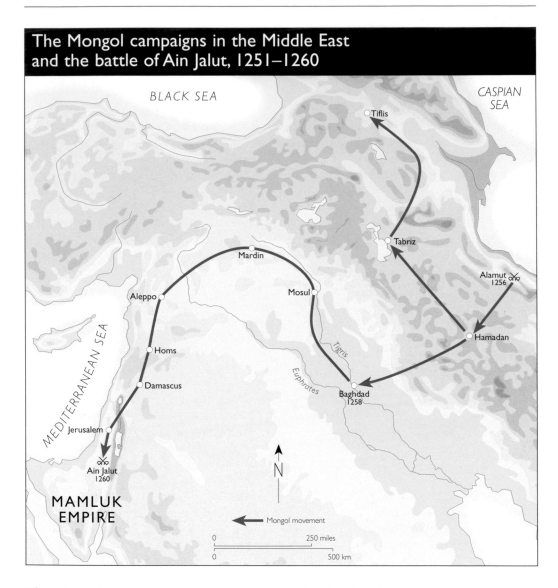

The Mongol campaigns in the Middle East and the battle of Ain Jalut, 1251–1260

BLACK SEA

CASPIAN SEA

Tiflis

Tabriz

Mardin

Alamut 1256

Aleppo

Mosul

Hamadan

MEDITERRANEAN SEA

Homs

Tigris

Damascus

Euphrates

Baghdad 1258

Jerusalem

Ain Jalut 1260

MAMLUK EMPIRE

N

Mongol movement

0   250 miles

0   500 km

The siege of Xiangyang

The second phase of the overall strategy resulted in one of the greatest sieges of Chinese history at Xiangyang, where the Mongols besieged the Southern Song for five years in an operation during which much ingenuity was shown on both sides. Xiangyang (the present-day Xiangfan in Hubei) consisted of the twin cities of Xiangyang and Fancheng, which lay opposite each other across the Han river. They formed the northern outpost of the Southern Song, being their last bastion beyond the central basin of the Yangtze. Xiangyang withstood the sustained siege by

Khubilai Khan from 1268 to 1271 while being defiantly supplied by river boat. The Song vessels are very interesting in that they were paddle boats, their motive power being supplied by men working treadmills. Two heroic Song officers, Zhang Shun and Zhang Gui, led a relief convoy of a hundred paddle boats laden with supplies, but were intercepted by the Mongols during the night, with bales of burning straw providing artificial illumination from the banks.

In 1272 the Song showed further enterprise by building a pontoon bridge to link the two cities, but the Mongols countered with great ingenuity of their own, and constructed mechanical saws, operated probably from the treadmills of paddle boats, which cut the bridge into sections, after which it was burned! The Southern Song defenders also had thunder crash bombs – the defeat of the Jin by the Mongols had been an acute lesson to them – but there was a serious shortage of supply. Ten years earlier, an official, in a memorandum about his own town's defences, had complained that the Southern Song arsenal had once produced a couple of thousand thunder crash bombs a month, but that they now had only 85 in stock, together with 95 fire arrows and 105 fire lances, 'which is not sufficient for a mere hundred men, let alone a thousand, to use against an attack by the [Mongol] barbarians'.

Xiangyang appears to have been much better stocked by the time the siege began in 1268, and one thunder crash bomb at least caused a named casualty when a certain Mongol officer called Liu Xianying led the attack up scaling ladders against Fancheng. A thunder crash bomb thrown from a trebuchet exploded beside him causing a serious wound in his left thigh. The next time that we hear a mention of this same Liu his wound has healed and he is now involved in a simultaneous attack on the walls of the city and on another fleet of Southern Song paddle ships bringing supplies along the river. This action is most interesting because the accounts of it confirm that the Mongols now had thunder crash bombs of their own, 'which were thrown with great noise and with loud reports' so that on the Song ships 'they were up to the ankles in blood'. A successful provisioning operation of Xiangyang was carried out later on in the siege. This time the Southern Song ships were equipped with fire lances, siege crossbows and trebuchets shooting fire bombs, but thunder crash bombs are not recorded for this operation on either side.

Yet even when a river blockade was finally put in place and firmly maintained, the Mongol siege weapons of traction trebuchets, bombs and siege crossbows proved incapable of causing any real damage to the twin cities and their walls. Something stronger was needed, and this was supplied in the form of Muslim counterweight trebuchets and their operators, summoned to China from the lands of the West. It is interesting to note that the traction trebuchet had made its way from China to the West centuries earlier. Now it returned in a new and more terrifying form. The counterweight trebuchet had long been valued in Europe and the Middle East, having rapidly supplanted the traction trebuchet since its first recorded use in 1165. In 1291, 20 years after Xiangyang, its Muslim enthusiasts were to bring 92 counterweight trebuchets into action with devastating results against the crusader stronghold of Acre.

The actual design of these machines as they were used in China is by no means clear, but a description of the siege of Xiangyang written 30 years afterwards tells us:

When [the artillerists] wanted to hurl them to a greater range, they added weight [to the counterpoise] and set it further back [on the arm]; when they needed only a shorter distance, they set it forward, nearer [the fulcrum].

There is, however, an intriguing passage from the Southern Song side of the conflict, because in response to the Mongol advance the Song began making counterweight trebuchets of their own:

In 1273 the frontier cities had all fallen. But Muslim trebuchets were constructed with new and ingenious improvements, and different kinds became available, far better than those used before.

This could mean swinging counterweights more like the familiar European version, or the mysterious 'improvements' may simply refer to a comparison with traction trebuchets, as it would indeed be strange if Khubilai Khan's imported engineers had not made use of the best machines at their disposal.

Whatever the details of their design, the Muslim trebuchets were constructed at the

The site of Karakorum. (David Lambert)

Mongol capital – where Khubilai Khan attended some of the trials in person – and then transported to Xiangyang. This may have been done by dismantling the machines, although they could have been mounted on wheeled carriages. Projectiles could now be launched weighing 10 times more than any stone thrown hitherto, and one particular shot (perhaps exceeding 90 kg [200 lbs]) launched on target brought down the drum tower of Xiangyang with a noise like thunder. The commentator noted above wrote, 'the projectiles were several feet in diameter, and when they fell to the earth, they made a hole three or four feet deep.' Massive stone balls therefore triumphed where both old-fashioned traction trebuchets and modern explosives had failed.

The fall of the Song dynasty
Realising the tremendous advantage that he now possessed, Khubilai wasted no time in sending these new weapons against the Southern Song capital of Hangzhou. Bayan, one of the most gifted of all Mongol leaders, was chosen to lead the advance. He crossed

the Yangtze in January 1275 and met the Song forces in a series of battles where Mongol superiority in artillery made a decisive difference. Bayan went on to bombard and take Yangzhou, 'breaking down temples, towers and halls', and using soft-cased bombs as a signalling device. Bayan's army occupied one town after another, some surrendering as soon as the army came in sight with its fearsome counterweight trebuchets, and finally Hangzhou fell. In 1279 the last remnants of the Song dynasty were eliminated, and Khubilai Khan became the first emperor of the new Yuan (Mongol) dynasty. He ruled from Beijing, with his summer palace at Shangdu, the 'stately pleasure dome' of Xanadu that was to become legendary because of Coleridge's famous poem.

The Japanese theatre 1274–81

The first invasion of Japan
Japanese history proudly speaks of two Mongol invasions of Japan in 1274 and 1281, both of which were driven back by the bravery of the samurai and the intervention

The beach at Hakata in Japan where the Mongols landed in 1274. (Author's collection)

of the gods. The 1274 attack was, however, of very brief duration and bears comparison to the first phase of most of the Mongol operations described above, all of which began with a reconnaissance in force. The first Japanese operation was nonetheless carried out with a much larger army than would have been expected in a raid, although this was probably due to the added complications and dangers of having to cross water.

The above account of the conquest of the Southern Song indicates quite clearly that Mongol prowess at sea-crossing had moved on considerably since the days of Kanghwa and Croatia, but the most important factor in this arose directly from the final conquest of Korea, whose considerable maritime resources were now in Mongol hands. This meant that for the first time Khubilai Khan could seriously contemplate crossing the Tsushima Strait between Pusan and Japan's island of Tsushima with an army of invasion.

In early 1274 Khubilai Khan issued an order for the Koreans to build 900 ships which were to transport an advance force of about 5,000 Mongol troops, between 6,000 and 8,000 Koreans, and a main body of 15,000 Mongols, Chinese and Jurchens. The crews, almost half of whom were Korean, consisted of 15,000 men. The journey from Pusan took two weeks, during which the Mongol force ravaged the islands of Tsushima and Iki, and probably also raided the Japanese coast of Hizen province. Landfall was made in the sheltered Hakata Bay where the modern city of Fukuoka now stands. Mongol detachments came ashore at various sites around the bay.

In addition to attacks by phalanxes of troops and clouds of anonymous arrows, a unique feature of the Mongol attacks were the thunder crash bombs fired against the Japanese troops. The use of these bombs, presumably flung by traction trebuchets, is one of the best-known aspects of the Mongol invasions, and may be found illustrated on a very prominent section of the *Moko Shurai Ekotoba* (Mongol Invasion Scroll) which a certain Takezaki Suenaga had painted shortly after the war as proof of his achievements. The bomb is exploding in front of a mounted samurai, sending its contents towards him. An eye-witness described how these 'mighty iron balls' were flung, and 'rolled down the hills like cartwheels, sounded like thunder, and looked like bolts of lightning'. Another account, from the *Hachiman Gudokun* reads:

The commanding general kept his position on high ground, and directed the various detachments as need be with signals from hand drums. But whenever the Mongol soldiers took to flight, they sent iron bomb shells flying against us, which made our side dizzy and confused. Our soldiers were frightened out of their wits by the thundering explosions, their eyes were blinded, their ears deafened, so that they could hardly distinguish east from west.

By nightfall the Japanese had been driven back several miles inland to Dazaifu. The Mongols burned the Japanese dwellings, and also set fire to the great Hakozaki shrine. However, fortunately for the Japanese, the Mongols then chose not to spend the night on shore, but to return to their ships. With this tactical withdrawal the first invasion concluded, because the armies never again left their ships for Japanese soil. Instead, during the night a fierce storm blew up, severely damaging the fleet lying at anchor. The Mongols immediately set sail back to Korea, taking one full month over the journey, having suffered the loss of 13,000 dead, about one-third of their total, including one high-ranking Korean general who was drowned.

This abrupt end to the first invasion has led several scholars to question some of the accepted details of the engagement. The destruction of the fleet by bad weather, which was to occur on a grand scale in the second invasion of 1281, has been doubted, one authority pointing out that late November, when the invasion occurred, is out of the typhoon season. It is interesting to note that the *Hachiman Gudokun* does not mention a storm at all, and instead notes simply that the following morning the local people were surprised to find the terrible invaders completely gone except for one ship

that had run aground. Korean sources, however, speak of a natural disaster and a Japanese court diary notes:

I heard that just when the enemy ships, several tens of thousands in number, appeared on the sea, a sudden gale arose and sent them all back, leaving some of them on land. It is also said that Otomo Yoriyasu had captured more than fifty enemy soldiers, all of whom were to be kept in captivity and forwarded to Kyoto later. As for the typhoon, is it not a manifestation of divine protection?

The Mongol invasion of 1274 therefore lasted only one day, and lost one in three of its invading force. It is impossible to know how many of these were killed by the samurai swords and arrows of the defenders, but if the storm theory is to be discounted, the proportion must have been very high indeed. The bravery and martial skills of the samurai turned this major raid, no matter how brief it may have been planned to be, into a pyrrhic victory. Unsurprisingly, this is not how it appears in the Yuan sources. A biography of one Mongol general, Liu Fu-heng, speaks of him defeating a Japanese army of 100,000. Other sources note that the withdrawal was purely tactical because the Mongols had run out of arrows.

The second invasion of Japan

Khubilai Khan never saw the first invasion as a disaster, but the next few years found him preoccupied with the conquest of the Southern Song. The Japanese, by contrast, were on a state of alert. Religious services increased, and the symbolic Hakozaki shrine was rebuilt. Valiant warriors, some 120 in all, were rewarded, and a coastal guard was mounted. One measure that was never actually carried out was a planned raid by Japan on Korea to be led by the Kyushu general, Shoni Tsunesuke. That same year (1276) the construction began of a defensive

OPPOSITE Mongol cruelty on the island of Iki as depicted on the Nichiren memorial statue at Hakata. (Author's collection)

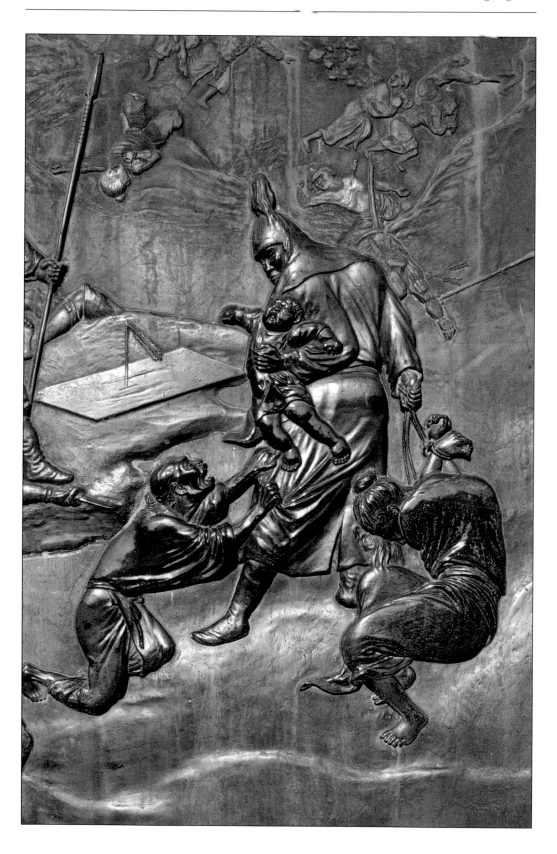

wall around Hakata Bay. The face of the wall looking out to sea was of stone and over 2 m (7 ft) high, while on the other side it sloped down along an earthen embankment.

The Mongol preparations were carried out on a much larger scale than in 1274, and we know from underwater archaeology that farming implements were included on board the ships, so the Mongols intended a permanent occupation of Japanese land. The newly available counterweight trebuchets do not appear to have been included in the plans for the second invasion, because when the commander of the fleet asked for technicians for Muslim trebuchets, his request was declined on the grounds that the machines were not suitable for naval warfare. Six hundred warships were ordered from southern China, in addition to 900 from Korea.

Two separate Mongol invasion fleets were ordered to join forces near Iki island. The Mongol general Arakhan was placed in supreme command, but the plan for the two

The Mongol wall at Hakata. (Richard Turnbull)

armies to join up before they attacked did not materialise. Instead the Eastern Route Army attacked Tsushima and Iki and then attempted to land in Hakata Bay. As before, the ferocity of the Japanese defence forced them back, so the Mongols established themselves on two islands in the bay, one of which, Shiga, was connected to the mainland by a narrow spit of land. From these islands they launched attacks against the Japanese for about a week. The Japanese responded with night raids against the Mongol ships. The Japanese boats, holding between 10 and 15 samurai, would close with a Mongol ship under cover of darkness, and lower its own mast to make a bridge for boarding. The samurai would then engage in hand-to-hand fighting with swords. On one occasion 30 samurai swam out to a Mongol ship, decapitated the entire crew, and then swam back. A certain Kusano Jiro led a raid in broad daylight and set fire to a ship even though his left arm was cut off. Kono Michiari also led a daytime raid with two boats. Thinking the Japanese were coming to

A wood carving of a samurai fighting a Mongol. (Author's collection)

surrender, the Mongols allowed them to come close, at which they were boarded and a high-ranking general was captured.

Attempts were also made to dislodge the Mongols from Shiga island. The Mongol response to the raids was to stretch chains between their ships and throw stones by catapults to sink the Japanese vessels. But at the end of this phase of the invasion the bravery of the samurai led the Mongol fleet to withdraw to Iki island, there to await the arrival of the southern Chinese contingent.

By the early part of the following month this second huge armada had begun arriving at various parts of the Japanese coast from the Goto islands in the west to Hakata. They eventually made rendezvous to the south of Iki, near the island of Takashima, where the Japanese launched a bold raid that deserves the title of 'battle' of Takashima. The fighting lasted a full day and night, but the Japanese were eventually driven off by sheer weight of numbers.

A massive attack on Hakata Bay now looked inevitable, but never happened,

The Mongol mound on Shiga island, erected by followers of Nichiren as a graveyard for the Mongols killed there during the invasion. (Author's collection)

The Mongol invasions of Japan, 1274–1281

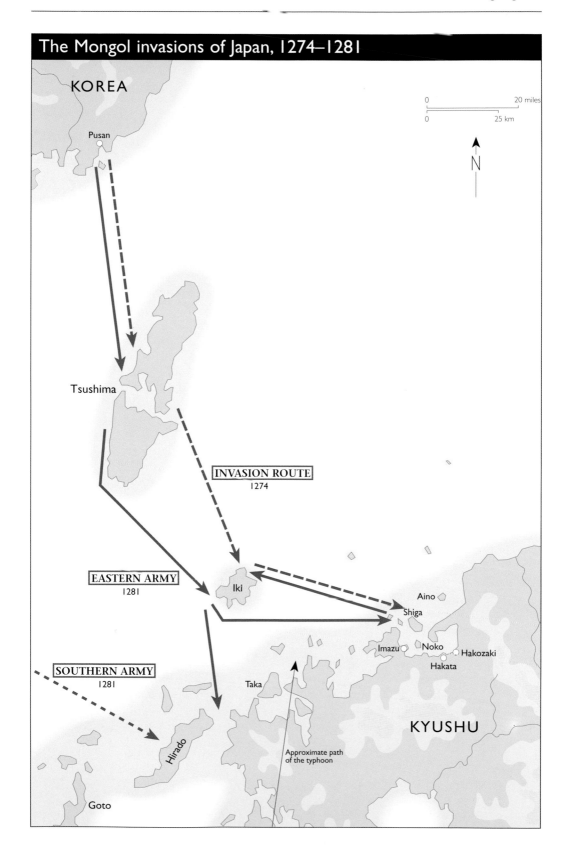

KOREA

Pusan

0   20 miles

0   25 km

N

Tsushima

INVASION ROUTE
1274

EASTERN ARMY
1281

Iki

Aino

Shiga

Imazu   Noko   Hakozaki
Hakata

SOUTHERN ARMY
1281

Taka

KYUSHU

Hirado

Approximate path
of the typhoon

Goto

because within days of the Japanese attack at Takashima a typhoon blew up. This was the famous *kamikaze*, the wind of the gods. Unlike the first typhoon, this one is well documented and was devastating in its effects. Korean casualties were 7,592 out of 26,989, nearly 30 per cent, but the Mongol and Chinese figures were much higher, between 60 and 90 per cent. Forced by the Japanese raids to stay in their ships, and unable to drop anchor in protected harbour waters, the Mongol fleet was obliterated. Tens of thousands of men were left behind with the wreckage as the remains of the fleet headed home, and most of these were killed in Japanese attacks during the next few days. A Chinese survivor left a valuable account:

First day: A hurricane wrecked our ships.

Fifth day: General Fan Wen-hu and others picked the best ships available and sailed away, leaving behind more than one hundred thousand officers and soldiers under the mountain [on Takashima]. After spending three days without food and without a commander we agreed to select Captain Chang as our commander and called him Governor Chang. Under his command we planned to cut trees and build ships for the purpose of returning home.

Seventh day: The Japanese attacked us and almost annihilated us. The remaining tens of thousands were captured and led away.

Ninth day: Arriving at Hakata, the Japanese killed all the Mongols, Koreans and the people of Han [northern Chinese]. They spared the lives of the newly submitted [i.e. southern Chinese] saying that they were the people of Tang and made them slaves instead. I, Chang, was one of them.

The failure of the Mongol invasions may partly be blamed on the Mongols' dependence on naval support from the conquered Koreans, who may well have been reluctant to give their all for their own conquerors. But to the Japanese the bravery of the samurai during the 'little ship' raids quickly became subsumed, and almost forgotten, under the gratitude for the divine gift of the *kamikaze*, whereby, to quote from a religious account, a 'divine storm rose in mighty force and scattered the enemy ships'. In fact no rewards were granted to samurai until 1286.

It is not generally known that a further Mongol invasion of Japan was planned between 1283 and 1285, for which an engineer was commissioned to build counterweight trebuchets to support the landings. Technicians were also drafted to the project, but as the invasion was cancelled what may have become a unique military experiment was never carried out. So the threat to Japan from overseas continued for many years, and in 1301 it was believed that an invasion fleet had been seen off the coast of Satsuma province. The samurai of the Hakata area providing coastal defences were taken off alert only in 1312.

The repulse of the Mongol invasions of Japan is comparable to the battle of Ain Jalut in that it represented a denial of the myth of unquestionable Mongol superiority. The events in Hakata Bay therefore hold a unique place in Japanese history. Through these battles the samurai spirit and the benevolence of the *kami* are combined in a way that expresses the spirit of Japan as does no other event in samurai history. After the Mongol invasions, the samurai went back to their time-honoured tradition of fighting each other. For these few years the samurai stood together.

Subadai Ba'adur (c1176–1248)

In most accounts of the Mongol conquests Genghis Khan's subordinates come over as two-dimensional characters, mounted automatons moving as stereotypically as the myth of Mongol supremacy would always have us believe. Yet in the service of Genghis Khan were many leaders of great military talent who were personalities in their own right. One of them was Subadai Ba'adur, whose name variously appears as Subedei, Sabatai, or Subodei. He was born in about 1176 the son of a blacksmith of the Uriangqadai clan and joined Temuchin's

Subadai Ba'adur was born in about 1176. He was one of Genghis Khan's most celebrated generals. This statue of him in Ulan Bator honours a fine soldier and a loyal and honourable follower of the Mongol Khans.
(David Lambert)

band when he was still a youth in about 1190. Along with his brother, Jelemei, Subadai rose quickly in Mongol service and commanded cavalry at the age of 25. Subadai appears to have been a heavyweight in more ways than one, and had to travel to battles in some form of carriage to spare the backs of the slight Mongol ponies!

Subadai is the exemplar of that remarkable and commendable loyalty shown by subordinate generals of the Mongols towards their ruling Khan. 'As felt protects from the wind,' he promised to Genghis Khan, 'so I will ward off your enemies.' His first independent command was in 1205–06 when he successfully pursued and killed Kutu and Chila'un, sons of the defeated Merki leader, Tokhto'a. Subadai commanded a *tumen* (10,000 men) in the wars against the

Xixia, and we read of him being given joint command of the 3,000 Mongols sent in pursuit of the Shah of Khwarazm after the Samarkand operation. When the Shah died in 1221, Subadai was one of the commanders entrusted with the reconnaissance mission 'to the Western lands' that took the Mongols into Russia for the first time.

This operation was a remarkable feat that brings great credit upon Subadai. Having destroyed several towns in Azerbaijan, the Mongols were bribed to spare Tabriz, and he and his men wintered in eastern Armenia. In 1221 the two generals defeated King Giorgi the Brilliant of Georgia near Tbilisi. From there they returned to Azerbaijan and were on the point of marching against Baghdad to destroy the Abbasid Caliphate, but instead returned to Georgia, defeating another Georgian army using the tactic of false retreat. They then swung north and advanced into southern Russia and captured Astrakhan. Pushing on across the river Don they penetrated the Crimean peninsula and were in the Ukraine to winter the snows of 1222–23. In 1223 they began to return home, only to be intercepted by an allied enemy force. These were the soldiers Subadai and his colleagues led to their deaths at the battle of the Kalka river.

Their earlier conquest of the territory of the Shah of Khwarazm had taken the Mongols as far as the borders of Azerbaijan, at which point Subadai and Jebe asked permission to proceed north and reconnoitre the 'Western lands'. This led to the conquest of Azerbaijan and Georgia, after which they came upon the nomadic Polovtsians, referred to in the chronicles as Kipchaks or Cumans (Kumans). By 1223 the Mongols had completed these operations and regrouped in the southern Russian steppes.

At that time what we now know as Russia and the Ukraine were ruled by a number of princes who jealously defended their own territories. These Russian princes would appear to have had no intelligence about the campaigns and conquests of Genghis Khan, and the first information that a new enemy had appeared in the southern steppes was brought to Mstislav Mstislavitch in Galich by his Polovtsian father-in-law, Khan Kotyan, whose nomadic territory lay close to the eastern most bend of the Dnieper. The *Chronicle of Novgorod* tells us:

He brought them numerous presents: horses, camels, buffaloes and girls. And he presented these gifts to them, and said the following, 'Today the Tartars took away our land and tomorrow they will come and take away yours.'

The name Tartars or Tatars is the expression often used in Russian source materials for the Mongol hordes. The original Tartars were a rival tribe wiped out by Genghis Khan, but the expression may also derive from *Tartarus* meaning 'Hell', the supposed origin of these strange warriors who had appeared from nowhere.

Mstislav of Galich immediately summoned a council of war in Kiev. The two other southern regional princes attended it: Mstislav Romanovich of Kiev and Mstislav Svyatoslavich of Chernigov. They made the decision that the Russians and Polovtsians should move east to seek out and destroy the Mongols wherever they might be found. When the expeditionary force was on its way the Mongol envoys met the main body at Pereyaslavl and tried to persuade them from fighting. But when a second attempt at parley failed the army crossed the Dnieper and marched eastwards across the steppes for nine days, little knowing that they had been misled by a Mongol false retreat conducted on a grand scale. Here they encountered a Mongol army at the Kalka river and were heavily defeated:

... his Kuman warriors failed, and retreated in such haste that they galloped over the Russian camp and trampled it underfoot. And there was not time for the Russian forces to form ranks. And so it came to complete confusion, and a terrible slaughter resulted.

Mstislav of Kiev defended himself inside a hastily erected stockade until he was persuaded to give himself up by Ploskyn, a Cossack leader fighting for the Mongols who swore 'on the holy cross' that Prince Mstislav would be released for ransom, but:

... this accursed Ploskyn lied, and he bound the princes hand and feet and turned them over to the Tartars. The princes were taken by the Tartars and crushed beneath platforms placed over their bodies on top of which the Tartars celebrated their victory banquet.

Following the death of Jebe on the return journey, Subadai successfully led the Mongol army home having covered around 6,500 km (4,000 miles) in less than three years.

Subadai may have served in Genghis Khan's last campaign against the Xixia, but the next action for which he is renowned was the successful siege of the Jin's southern capital of Kaifeng in 1232, where Subadai had to contend with thunder crash bombs thrown by catapult. That was the last Subadai was to see of campaigning in China, although in 1257 his son, Uriyangkhadai, led an army into the country now known as Vietnam, and his grandson, Bayan, was to accomplish the destruction of the Southern Song in 1276.

Subadai's last and greatest campaign was the invasion of Russia and eastern Europe, described in detail above. Batu, son of Jochi, was the overall leader, but Subadai was the actual commander in the field, and as such was present in both the northern and southern campaigns against Russia and the Ukraine. He commanded the central column that moved against Hungary. While Kaidu's northern force won the battle of Leignitz and Kadan's army triumphed in Transylvania, Subadai was waiting for them on the Hungarian plain. The newly reunited army then withdrew to the Sajo river where they inflicted the tremendous defeat on King Bela IV at the battle of Mohi. Subadai masterminded the operation, and it was to prove one of his greatest victories.

The king had summoned a council of war at Gran, an important settlement on the south of the Danube bend upstream from Buda and Pest. As Batu was advancing on Hungary from the north-east it was decided to concentrate at Pest and then head north-east to confront the Mongol army. When news of the Hungarians' apparent intentions reached the Mongol commanders they slowly withdrew, drawing their enemies on. The Mongols took a stand near Eger to the east of the river Sajo, on a flat plain bounded to the north by the famous wine-growing area of Tokay. It was a strong position. Woodland prevented their ranks from being reconnoitred, while across the river on the plain of Mohi, the Hungarian army appeared to be very exposed.

Subadai launched the battle of Mohi during the night of 10–11 April 1241, only one day after his compatriots had won the great battle of Leignitz. One division crossed the river in secret to advance on the Hungarian camp from the south-east. The main body began to cross the Sajo by the bridge at Mohi. This met with some resistance, so catapults were used to clear the opposite bank. When the crossing was completed the other contingent attacked at the same time. The result was panic, and to ensure that the Hungarians did not fight desperately to the last man the Mongols left an obvious gap in their encirclement. As they had planned, the fleeing Hungarians poured through this opened trap which led to a swampy area. When the Hungarian knights split up, the light Mongol archers picked them off at will and it was later noted that corpses littered the countryside for the space of a two days' journey. Two archbishops and three bishops were killed at the Sajo. By late 1241 Subadai was discussing plans to invade Austria, Italy and Germany, when the news came of the death of Ogodei Khan, and the Mongols withdrew.

With his return to Mongolia Subadai's name disappears from history. Perhaps he retired from active service, because we know he was dead by 1248. He remains one of Genghis Khan's most celebrated generals, and there is a statue of him in Ulan Bator, honouring a fine soldier and a loyal and honourable follower of the Mongol Khans.

Terror and reality

Throughout all the accounts of the Mongol conquests we can discern in the background an echo of great human suffering. Ordinary people from Poland to Java, who under any other circumstances might have lived lives that may have been short but were certainly uneventful, suddenly found their world turned upside down by a horde of demons apparently let loose from the depths of Hell. As Juvaini put it so well, describing one such eruption:

And they were heedless of the disorder and unrest prevailing in the world and of Fate's assault and battery of her creatures, great and small, until suddenly they beheld a small troop of horsemen like a puff of smoke, who arrived before the gates of the town ...

A civilian massacre was the almost inevitable accompaniment to a Mongol triumph. There were exceptions when only the members of a garrison were killed, but thousands of men, women and children died at Mongol hands. For example, Juvaini tells us that at Merv:

The people of Merv were then distributed among the soldiers and levies, and in short, to each man was allocated the execution of three to four hundred persons ... So many had been killed by nightfall that (by comparison) the mountains became hillocks, and the plain was soaked with the blood of the mighty.

Also, according to Juvaini, when one woman at Tirmiz concealed a pearl by swallowing it, Genghis Khan ordered that his men should rip open the bellies of the slain. In Herat 'no head was left on a body nor body with a head', and at Nishapur the destruction was greater than usual because of the revenge for the death of Genghis Khan's son-in-law, Toghachar. After taking away the craftsmen, as was customary:

They severed the heads of the slain from their bodies and heaped them up in piles, keeping those of the men separate from those of the women and children ... Flies and wolves feasted on the breasts of sadrs; eagles on mountain tops regaled themselves with the flesh of delicate women; vultures banqueted on the throats of houris.

The cities of central Asia appear to have suffered no more than two Mongol attacks for them to be utterly destroyed. By contrast, in the European theatre it was often the case that most destruction at Mongol hands was caused by repeated raids, rather than one cataclysmic invasion. Krakow was burned in 1241, but rebuilt only to suffer more Mongol attacks by the Golden Horde, one of which has provided one of Krakow's most poignant local customs. When the Mongols were spotted, a trumpeter raised the alarm from the tower, but a Mongol arrow pierced him through the throat. To this day the playing of the same trumpet call from the same tower, but finishing abruptly at the precise note and moment when the watchman was struck dead, commemorates the event.

Although the voices of the chroniclers of different cultures all paint similar apocalyptic scenes of Mongol destruction, less familiar are accounts of the process of rebuilding and renewal. For example, the capture of Vladimir involved the burning of the Cathedral of the Assumption when the populace sheltered in it. We are told that during the siege many terrified people fled for sanctuary to the church, which they locked behind them, and climbed up to the choir loft. The Mongols:

... began to search after the princes and their mother, and found that they were inside the church ... The Tartars broke the gates of the church and slaughtered those

When the Mongols were spotted approaching Krakow a trumpeter raised the alarm from the tower, but a Mongol arrow pierced him through the throat. This event is still commemorated today. (Ian Clark)

who were inside and resisted. And they began to ask the whereabouts of the princes and their mother and found that they were in the choir loft. They began to entice them to come down, but they did not listen to them. The Tartars then brought many fire logs inside the church and set it on fire. Those present in the choir loft, praying, gave their souls to God; they were burned and joined the list of martyrs, and the Tartars pillaged the holy church and they tore the miracle-making icon of the Mother of God.

In spite of such a dramatic account the destruction cannot have been too great because the following year it became the venue for Grand Prince Yuri's funeral. Somehow most of the places eventually recovered, and to the frequent civilian experience of Mongol depredations must be added the unexpected phenomenon of Mongols as protectors. This was certainly how some Christian groups in the Middle East regarded the Mongols. When the Mongols conquered Syria they accorded their new Christian subjects the same status as the Muslims, thus giving the Christians a welcome break from religious persecution. Unfortunately, the Christians of Damascus in particular, who regarded the Mongol victory over the Muslims as just retribution, responded to this state of affairs with arrogance and contempt, going so far as to 'ring bells and cause wine to flow even in the mosque of the Umayyads'. So when the news of the Mongol defeat at Ain Jalut reached Damascus the stores and houses of Christians were attacked and looted in retaliation.

It is quite clear that the terror inspired by the Mongol name was deliberately used as a psychological weapon. On many occasions survivors of Mongol massacres were allowed to escape to the Mongol's next target so that their tales would spread terror. This might even result in the surrender of a town before the Mongols had actually been seen, and in this context it is interesting to note the ease with which Genghis Khan captured cities in the central Asian Muslim world compared to similar operations in China. The Chinese had learned to live with nomad hordes over the centuries and were used to their ways, but to the subjects of the Khwarazm Shah, the Mongols were strange, alien savages, and it was this 'barbarian factor' that Genghis Khan exploited so well.

To capture a Khwarazm city the Mongols would round up the male population of the surrounding districts and drive them at sword-point against ditch and wall. Sometimes these unwilling 'forlorn hope' troops were disguised as Mongols, with a Mongol flag to every 10 men, so that a garrison would believe itself to be threatened by an overwhelming Mongol army. This is exactly how prisoners from Bukhara were used to besiege Samarkand, and the Samarkand captives in turn were driven against Urgench.

The fate of Bukhara and its inhabitants came to represent the comparatively lenient treatment the Mongols were willing to mete out to a place that had not put up a stout resistance against them. The population was driven out and the men taken into Mongol service, while only the members of the military garrison were slaughtered. As Juvaini puts it:

Of the Qanqli [Turks] no male was spared who stood higher than the butt of a whip and more than thirty thousand were counted amongst the slain; while their small children, the children of the nobles and their womenfolk, slender as the cypress, were reduced to slavery. When the town and the citadel had been purged of rebels and the walls and outworks levelled with the dust, all the inhabitants of the town, men and women, ugly and beautiful, were driven out on to the field.

The city was then set on fire, deliberately, according to Juvaini, but the wooden houses were so tightly packed together that it was almost inevitable that a conflagration would accompany the sack.

... and the people of Bukhara, because of the desolation, were scattered like the constellation of the Bear and departed into the villages, while the site of the town became 'like a level plain'.

This concluding phrase, a quotation from the Koran, was to be used time and again in accounts of Mongol victories.

News also spread much wider than the actual area of a campaign. But in the absence of modern means of communication the depredations of the Mongols came to the ears of the inhabitants of distant countries only as travellers' tales, formal ambassadorial reports, or through unusual disruptions to the annual routine. For example, it was in 1238 that the first inkling reached England that something terrible was happening far away to the east. The incident was rather mundane, and the chronicler Matthew Paris relates that:

The inhabitants of Gotland and Friesland, dreading their attacks, did not, as was their custom, come to Yarmouth in England at the time of the herring fisheries, at which place their ships usually loaded; and, owing to this, herrings in that year were considered of no value, on account of their abundance.

The confusion in Matthew Paris's mind is indicated by his assumption that the merchants of the Low Countries and the Baltic were themselves under threat from the Mongols, whereas it was their trading links with Novgorod that had been severed by the Russian campaign. This caused repercussions as far down the supply chain as England, and as a result there was no market for the glut of herring. In such ways were the fishmongers of Norfolk linked by an invisible causal chain to decisions made on the steppes of central Asia, the strangest illustration of all of Mongol 'chaos theory' in action.

OPPOSITE Many terrified people fled to the Cathedral of the Assumption in Vladimir; they locked the door behind them, and climbed up to the choir loft. But the Mongols set fire to the building. (Author's collection)

The sage Changchun 1148–1227

There can have been no more unpopular position in the Mongol court than that of ambassador. Time and again we read that the pretext for a Mongol invasion was the mutilation or execution of a Mongol envoy. As Giovanni di Piano Carpini put it so succinctly, 'Now it is the custom of the Tartars never to make peace with men who kill their envoys until they have taken vengeance on them.'

Those who took these hazardous roles hardly lived lives long enough for one of their number to be included under our heading of 'portrait of a civilian'. By contrast, however, those who attended the Mongol court as ambassadors from other lands were invariably well treated. The famous envoys sent to Karakorum by the Pope sent back descriptions of the Mongols that are well known and historically very valuable. However, instead of these celebrated figures I shall present one who is comparatively little known, yet whose achievement in becoming a close confidante of Genghis Khan himself was almost unparalleled.

The visitor's name was Changchun ('Eternal Spring'), and his most unusual claim to fame was that he was believed to be 300 years old. Changchun was one of those remarkable figures who unite history with mythology: a legendary Chinese Taoist sage who was renowned for having discovered the secret of eternal life. It is therefore not surprising to read that in 1219 Genghis Khan, who had heard the reputation of Changchun, gave orders for the sage to be brought to him. The Khan was no longer young and years of battle had made him fearful for his own mortality, so what was more natural that the Universal Lord of Heaven should now seek to know the mystery of the elixir of life?

The man given the responsibility of finding Changchun and persuading him to visit Genghis Khan was called Liu Zhonglu. He was one of the Khan's most trusted advisers. So important was his mission that Liu was given a golden tablet on which was inscribed a message giving him full authority to act in the name of Genghis Khan. Liu Zhonglu's outward journey was an epic in itself, because he had to cross the territory where the wars between the Mongols and the Jin were still continuing, and over a year passed before Liu finally made contact with Changchun.

By 1220 the object of Liu's tremendous endeavour was not in fact 300 years old, but a more modest 72, when he received the summons that had taken so long to reach him. Changchun shrank from the prospect of such a long journey to meet the terrible conqueror, but such was the authority of Genghis Khan that Changchun set out on an epic journey that was to take him four years and must have tested his physical and spiritual resources to the utmost.

'He sat with the rigidity of a corpse, stood with the stiffness of a tree, moved swift as lightning and walked like a whirlwind,' wrote the author of the preface to *Travels of an Alchemist*, the work that related the sage's journey to the Great Khan. In it we read fascinating descriptions of scenery and people as Changchun makes his peaceful way through northern China and the steppe lands of the nomads. We hear of the sight of the mountains south of Lake Baikal, of the travellers' first meetings with Muslims, and of an escort provided by the future Khan Ogodei to help them negotiate steep mountain slopes. Towards the end of 1221 the party neared Samarkand, where only a quarter of the previous population now remained following the Mongol victory, but enough of the place was intact for Changchun to be installed in the comfort of the former palace of the Khwarazm Shah. As

Genghis Khan was still some distance away on his campaigns in pursuit of Jalal-al-Din, Changchun was grateful to be allowed to spend the winter in Samarkand.

In April 1222 a message arrived from Genghis Khan expressing pleasure at the news of Changchun's safe arrival. Genghis Khan was then encamped near Kabul, and the snow in the passes over the Hindu Kush was still 'deeper than the length of a whip', but, with an experienced Mongol escort to guide him, Changchun moved on and finally arrived in the presence of Genghis Khan in May. Almost immediately the crucial question was posed. Genghis Khan asked Changchun what medicines of eternal life he had brought with him. The sage replied, 'I have the means of protecting life, but no elixir that will prolong it.' Genghis Khan did not allow himself to display any disappointment, but treated Changchun with every kindness and consideration.

Months of conversations followed between the sage and the conqueror of Asia. Genghis Khan listened patiently to Changchun's teachings on morality and government, much of which must have been unpalatable to his tastes. Changchun certainly did not mince words when he criticised aspects of Mongol culture and customs. This included a great disapproval of hunting – the Mongol passion – and much

advice on sexual restraint, which Changchun recommended to Genghis Khan as the nearest approximation to the elixir he so desired. But Genghis Khan clearly regarded Changchun as heaven-sent and ordered his teachings to be written down and preserved.

The Khan was very reluctant to allow the old man to return to China when the months of audiences had passed, but Changchun insisted, and shortly before the two men parted Genghis Khan enquired as to how many disciples the sage had in China. The interpreter replied that there were many, because he had seen their names on the tax rolls. Genghis Khan therefore issued an imperial decree exempting all the sage's pupils from taxation. Changchun left for home in the spring of 1223, and took less time on the return journey by being guided on the shorter route across the Gobi desert. Following Changchun's safe return to China, Genghis Khan entrusted him with the administration of all the monks in China.

The two men never met again, and in fact both died in the same year of 1227, having experienced one of the most remarkable meetings of minds in world history. Future ambassadors to the court of the Khan would come and go, but no visit would ever be quite the same as the encounter between Genghis Khan and the man whom he believed possessed the secret of eternal life.

The jungle frontiers

Reference has been made throughout this work to the Mongols' capacity to adopt, adapt and survive amidst changing and challenging military situations. The harshest lessons of all were provided by the campaigns by which the Mongol Empire expanded to its fullest extent. With the Mongol campaigns in south-east Asia we may say that the war ended.

The Mongol targets were the warm and humid lands now known as Burma, Thailand, Cambodia, Vietnam and Indonesia, with their dense jungles, long rivers, insects and diseases. These operations were to become Khubilai Khan's last efforts at Mongol conquest and encapsulated all the challenges of sea transport, climate, environment, temperature and unfamiliar styles of warfare that had already tested the myth of Mongol invincibility.

The Vietnamese campaigns

In 1253, in a successful bid to outflank the Southern Song, Khubilai Khan had annexed the province of Yunnan, destroying the Nanzhao kingdom based at its capital of Dali. The operation was conducted by Uriyangkhadai, the son of the famous Subadai. In 1257 Uriyangkhadai led another army across the border into the country now known as Vietnam. At the time of the Mongols it was divided into two kingdoms: Annam in the north, with its capital at Hanoi, and Champa in the south. So rapid was the Mongol advance that the Annamese king fled to an offshore island, and in 1258 recognised Mongol authority by sending his son as hostage to the Khan's court.

Twenty years later the king of Champa received a command to pay homage and, no doubt recalling the fate of his northern neighbour, agreed immediately to send an annual tribute of 20 elephants. In 1281, however, his successor, King Jaya Indravarman IV, aroused Mongol wrath by refusing to continue the humiliating exercise. Khubilai Khan responded by sending Sodu, one of his leading officials, on a punitive expedition by sea. Sodu, commanding a force of 100 ships and 5,000 men, landed on the Champa coast, but the Cham king withdrew to the mountains and led a fierce guerrilla war that prevented the Mongols from making any headway.

War elephants would also probably have played a part, although not on the Mongol side, because the annual tribute of 20 beasts is likely to have provided only a prestige form of travel for exalted personages. In Vietnam, war elephants were an established feature of local military practice. Vietnamese elephants carried only one warrior, along with a mahout, and the elephants themselves are described as taking an active role in any fighting. They caught foot soldiers in their trunks to hurl them into the air and attacked enemy elephants using their tusks.

An interesting addition to the elephant armoury is also likely to have been used against Sodu. In 1171 a Chinese official had journeyed to Champa and taught the art of warfare using mounted crossbow men to the Chams, who put the technique into practice, both on horseback and on elephants. The latter arrangement involved a two-man artillery crew with a double-bow crossbow on the back of an elephant, a technique used against the Khmer kingdom of Cambodia in 1177. Bas reliefs of these weapons in action appear at the Bayon of Angkor Thom and, as these detailed illustrations were carved only a century before Khubilai Khan invaded Champa, it is highly likely that such weapons were also brought to bear against

Mongol horsemen crossing a river. (Author's collection)

the Mongols. The Chams had also a considerable knowledge of fortification, and an early Chinese text described walls 9 m (30 feet) high pierced with loopholes.

Whatever the techniques used, Cham resistance forced Khubilai Khan to seek the co-operation of Annam against its neighbour, but its king, Tran Thanh-ton, was not keen to allow Mongol horsemen to cross his territories, even though he was still sending embassies to the Mongol court. So he too resisted the Mongol invaders. Once again guerrilla raids took their toll, and the heat and heavy rains caused an outbreak of pestilence in the Mongol ranks. Finally, at a decisive battle at Siming in the summer of 1285, the Mongols were defeated and Sodu was killed.

A second expedition attacked Annam again in 1286 and reached Hanoi by 1287. The city was captured and the Annamese king fled once again. Not satisfied with his victory, Toghon unwisely returned during the hot season of 1288. This time a fierce naval battle took place in the estuary of the Bach Dang river off Haiphong, where a celebrated Vietnamese general had defeated a Chinese army several centuries before. General Tran

Hung Dao now repeated the victory, using the same tactics, against the Mongols. He waited until high tide, and lured the Mongol fleet into advancing over an area of shallow water where iron-tipped stakes had been planted. When the tide turned the Mongol ships were caught on the projections, and suffered great losses. On land, too, they were forced to retreat because of the heat and the environment, much to Khubilai's anger, and the efforts to conquer Vietnam were effectively over. Yet both kings sensibly realised that Mongol attacks might continue unless they made some form of token tribute. So Annam and Champa formally acquiesced to Mongol authority, which, as they had correctly anticipated, meant that they were simply left alone. This was not the fate of the much less diplomatically minded king of Burma, whose sorry story will now be related.

The Mongol invasion of Burma

In 1271 the Yunnan government in Dali was used by Khubilai Khan to demand tribute from the king of Burma. The present incumbent of the post was King Narathihapate, who was described on a pagoda that he erected in his

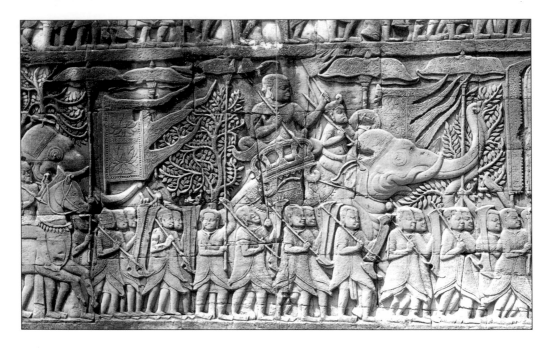

Khmer war elephants as depicted on the walls of the Bayon at Angkor Thom. Such animals were used against the Mongols in Burma. (Peter Danford)

own honour as 'the supreme commander of a vast army of 36 million soldiers, and the swallower of 300 dishes of curry every day'! He was also reputed to have 3,000 concubines, but this item was omitted from the public inscription. The Yunnan ambassadors were sent back empty-handed, but others returned in 1273 with a letter from the Mongol Khan himself. As the new ambassadors did not take their shoes off sufficiently often in the king's presence, he had them executed. Not surprisingly, the Yunnanese reported to Khubilai Khan that war would be the only way to bring these stubborn people to their senses. The Mongols were, however, preoccupied with other matters (it was the year before the invasion of Japan) so no action was taken against Burma until 1277, when an unwise raid by the Burmese across the Chinese border made a response inevitable.

In that same year Khubilai Khan ordered Nasir al-Din, the son of his trusted Muslim retainer, Saiyid Ajall, to lead an expedition against the Burmese capital of Pagan. Once more a Mongol army had to face unfamiliar fighting conditions. On this occasion we know for certain that they were confronted by war elephants because a lively and detailed account was produced by that great traveller and confidante of the Mongol court: Marco Polo. His description of the battle of Ngasaungyyan in 1277 actually compresses a decade of history into one episode and contains certain errors of location and numbers, but the overall impression of what happened is probably quite accurate and provides a unique insight into this latest challenge to the Mongol myth of mobile invincibility.

The Mongols then continued their advance into Burma, but the jungle environment and the heat finally exhausted them and they returned to China. The Burmese king, however, does not seem to have learned anything from his defeat, because 1283 was to find him raiding China once again. In 1287 Khubilai Khan sent a further expedition under his grandson, Temur, against this 'insolent king'. The temperature and the humidity must again have been a trial, but they pressed on until King Narathihapate fled and his city of Pagan was sacked. Perhaps it was the ease with which Pagan was finally taken that lies at the root of Marco Polo's yarn about Khubilai Khan telling his 'gleemen and jugglers' to go and take Burma.

The Mongol invasion of Java

Java was the most far-flung destination of all the Mongol campaigns in south-east Asia. Just as in the Burmese and Vietnamese situations, the process began with Khubilai Khan sending an envoy demanding homage from King Kertanagara, the ruler of Java, who responded by branding the ambassador's face. The subsequent Mongol expedition, which set out in 1292, was therefore intended to avenge this grave insult. A large naval force comparable to that used against Japan 11 years earlier carried out the invasion. The fleet set sail from Quanzhou (the place that Marco Polo calls Daytoun) and took several months to reach Java because they chose an open-sea route, calling at small islands, rather than one that followed the coast through Malacca and Sumatra. We are told that 'the wind was strong and the sea very rough, so that the ships rolled heavily and the soldiers could not eat for many days.'

The Mongols landed early in 1293 near to present-day Rembang on the north-eastern coast of Java. The Mongol commander landed half his army here and instructed them to march overland in a show of force, while the rest of the troops continued eastwards by sea. Their rendezvous point was Surabaya, where the river, which provided the orientation for the land forces, entered the sea. The two armies joined up around the beginning of May, and the land party expressed surprise that they had met with so little resistance as they crossed a landscape already scarred by recent fighting. An explanation was soon forthcoming. A Javanese rebel had taken advantage of the turmoil caused by the Mongols' arrival and had overthrown and killed King Kertanagara. Kertanagara's son-in-law, Prince Vijaya, was carrying on the struggle in the south of the country near present-day Kediri, which accounted for the absence of Javanese troops in the north. Hoping to use the Mongol army to help him crush the rebels, Prince Vijaya sent envoys to assure the invaders that he had already pledged the homage that his late father-in-law had so steadfastly refused.

The envoys also acquainted the Mongols with all the details they needed of the roads, rivers and resources of the country to enable them to march to Vijaya's assistance. Some rebel troops tried to stop them moving upstream from Surabaya, but were easily routed and fled into the interior. The Chinese account tells us:

The commanders of the [Mongol] imperial army made a camp in the form of a crescent on the bank of the river and left the ferry in charge of a commander of ten thousand; the fleet in the river and the cavalry and infantry on shore then advanced together, and Hi Ning-kuan [a Javanese commander], seeing this, left his boat and fled overnight, whereupon more than a hundred large ships, with devils' heads on the stem, were captured.

The Mongol army continued on its way upriver and fought a battle under the walls of Modjopait (Majapahit), the strongpoint (and future capital) where Vijaya was holding out, and drove a further rebel army back into the jungle. Finally, the Mongols moved on to the rebels' base at the fortified town of Daha (modern Kediri) and destroyed the final opposition to Vijaya. This action is of some historical interest because the chronicle tells us that, in order to co-ordinate their attack, the separate Mongol and loyalist Javanese units agreed to commence battle when they heard the sound of the *pao*. This word was originally used to identify a catapult, and later a cannon, but its use here referring to a signalling device indicates that these would have been thunderclap bombs – explosive gunpowder devices cased in thick paper which acted like a maroon. The bombs were fitted with a time fuse, and one would probably have been flung up into the air from a traction trebuchet. Its loud bang would then have been the signal to advance.

Prince Vijaya then took an enormous gamble. As his enemies were destroyed he no longer had need of a Mongol army to help him, and he was also very reluctant to reward them for their efforts. He therefore

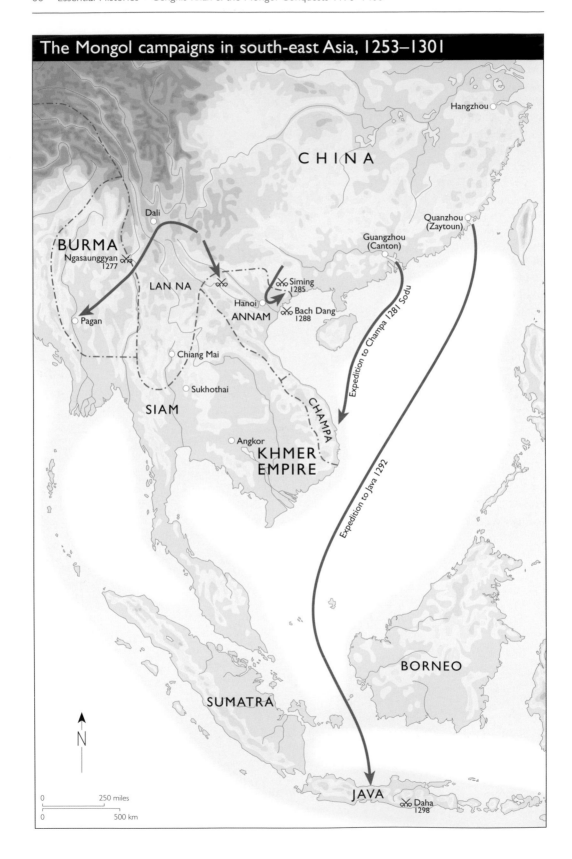

The Mongol campaigns in south-east Asia, 1253–1301

CHINA

Hangzhou

Dali

BURMA

Ngasaunggyan
1277

LAN NA

Quanzhou
(Zaytoun)

Guangzhou
(Canton)

Siming
1285

Hanoi

Bach Dang
1288

ANNAM

Pagan

Chiang Mai

Sukhothai

Expedition to Champa 1281 Sodu

CHAMPA

SIAM

Angkor

KHMER
EMPIRE

Expedition to Java 1292

BORNEO

SUMATRA

N

0   250 miles

0   500 km

JAVA   Daha
1298

made up an excuse for having to return to his capital, and was escorted by a small detachment of Mongol soldiers. On the way back he repudiated his homage, slaughtered the guards, and moved into a hostile position against the Mongols. An army was quickly sent against him, which he successfully ambushed, causing the survivors to flee back towards the coast.

Here the Mongols rapidly considered their position. They had been in Java for four months, and were already suffering from the equatorial heat, so, taking with them what prisoners and treasure they had gained, the fleet set sail for China and home. Three thousand Mongols perished in the Java expedition, and even the treasure, which included gold, silver and rhinoceros horn, was not sufficient to save the campaign commander from receiving 17 lashes and having one-third of his property confiscated. In 1287 Khubilai Khan went to war against a rebel Mongol commander called Nayan and commanded on the battlefield from a splendid palanquin mounted on the backs of four elephants. This was evidence indeed of a certain cultural borrowing from the lands of south-east Asia, his boldest initiative.

The submission of Siam

The place we now know as Thailand consisted at the time of the Mongols of a number of separate states. King Ramkhamhaeng of Siam, whose capital was at Sukhothai in the south, took a very different approach to the Mongol Empire from that of his Burmese or Javanese contemporaries, and deliberately cultivated good relations with Khubilai Khan. The king, who was in fact the first Thai monarch to receive the now legendary present of a white elephant, negotiated a treaty of amity with Mongol China in 1282 and made a personal visit to Khubilai Khan shortly before the Great Khan died in 1294. History does not record whether or not elephants, of any colour, changed hands, but the process saved Siam from the invasions suffered by its neighbours.

One reason for Ramkhamhaeng's success was that he was protected to the north by the northern Thai kingdom of Lan Na, ruled

King Ramkhamhaeng of Siam deliberately cultivated good relations with Khubilai Khan. The king negotiated a treaty of amity with Mongol China in 1282 and made a personal visit to Khubilai Khan, as shown here in this crude Thai illustration. (Author's collection)

by King Mangrai. This monarch had but recently consolidated his position by warfare, and his capital of Chiang Mai was only founded in 1296. Mangrai was acutely aware of the Mongol threat, as his territory touched the Chinese border, but actual hostilities with Mongol China began only in 1296 at Lan Na's northern tip, where a border dispute turned into war. However, an expedition against Lan Na, carried out in 1301, proved to be another Mongol disaster.

The only kingdom not to be mentioned so far is what remained of the once glorious Khmer Empire of Cambodia, the creator of the wonderful temples, shrines and palaces of Angkor. A Yuan ambassador went to Cambodia in 1296 and left a celebrated and valuable description of Angkor Thom. He suffered neither ill treatment nor contempt, and his writings about the buildings tell us that 'inside the palace are many marvellous places, but the defences are very severe and it is impossible to enter.' Yet the security was illusory, because by this time much of the country ruled from there had been overrun by the Thais. This was the rationale behind

King Ramkhamhaeng's soothing approaches to the Mongol court. While the Mongols continued to threaten or even destroy his enemies in Burma and Vietnam and kept his Thai ally and rival to the north in a state of concern, the King of Siam could prosper at the expense, chiefly, of the Khmers of Cambodia. His kingdom, after all, owed its very existence to the capture of Sukhothai from the Khmer governor in 1220. It would be a century and a half before Angkor finally fell to the Siamese in 1431, but such a far-sighted strategy by the Siamese king would surely have been one of which the great despot Khubilai Khan would have approved.

The peaceful submission of Siam marked the conclusion of the Mongol conquest of south-east Asia. Khubilai Khan died shortly after meeting the Siamese king, having had the satisfaction of seeing the Mongol Empire expand to this, its final extent. For the grandson of Genghis Khan the war really had ended.

Khubilai Khan mounted on an elephant. (Author's collection)

The Mongol legacy

Khubilai Khan died in 1294, not as a nomad horseman in a felt tent, but as the emperor of China, ruler of a Mongol empire that had evolved enormously from the entity he had inherited. He could look back on a lifetime of conquest, when Mongol warriors had been in action from Poland to Palestine and from Kiev to Korea, but of all the campaigns he and his predecessors had conducted, none had been so colossal nor so transforming as the 70-year-long learning exercise that had encompassed the Mongol conquest of China. From there he had gone on to create what would be within the space of one century an empire that spanned much of the known world. The process had begun with a nomad leader using tried and tested tactics against unfamiliar enemies and ended with a Chinese emperor despatching huge fleets to distant lands.

The Mongol dynasties

At the beginning of the 14th century, this great empire stood defined by the individual dynasties which the sons and grandsons of Genghis Khan had established as their inheritance. Most splendid of all was the Yuan dynasty of China, founded by Khubilai Khan. In Persia ruled the Ilkhans, whose hegemony had been founded by Hulegu, Khubilai's brother, who died in 1265. Another of Genghis Khan's grandsons, Batu, who died in 1255, had become the ruler of the Golden Horde in Russia, while the Jagatai khanate, named after Genghis Khan's second son, lorded it over the remains of the Khwarazm Empire. There is no space in this book to give an adequate account of the dissolution of these great sub-empires, but certain points may be covered because of the light they shine on the processes whereby the Mongol Empire was originally created.

Genghis Khan is credited with having warned his successors not to forget their hardy steppe origins and be seduced by the luxury and pleasures of a sedentary society, so in some ways the break-up of the Mongol Empire in China, Persia and Russia is almost a mirror image of the epic involved in creating it. Genghis Khan's apocryphal statement was a particularly acute observation in the Chinese context, and Temur (1294–1307), Khubilai's successor, was the last able member of the Yuan dynasty. Khubilai had embraced Chinese civilisation as a means of enriching the Mongol world both politically and militarily, but his descendants succumbed to all its vices. After Temur's death there were fierce succession disputes, and the perception of weakness and debauchery among their rulers encouraged Chinese patriots to stir up rebellion in the name of shedding an alien yoke.

In 1356 the most successful of these rebels, Zhu Yuanzhang, the future Ming emperor, seized Nanjing from the Yuan and made it his capital. The Mongol court seemed at first to be indifferent to the loss of southern China, which they had so recently and so laboriously acquired from the Southern Song, but then other rebels arose against their neglect, until Zhu Yuanzhang realised that he was fighting a divided and demoralised foe. In 1368 a Mongol prince died gallantly trying to defend the capital against the Ming advance. The last Yuan emperor died in 1370. His last words are said to have been, 'What evil I have committed to lose my empire thus!'

Over in the south-west of Asia, Hulegu had died in 1265 in the knowledge that he had failed to add Syria and Egypt to the Mongol Empire. His successors were the Ilkhans of Persia, who embraced both Islam and civilisation with equal enthusiasm.

Under Ghazan, their capital of Tabriz began to flourish, and as the historian Rashid ad-Din put it in glorious hyperbole, 'The Mongols, who until then had only destroyed, now began to build.' But the price for this was the abandonment of the hard Mongol heritage warned of by Genghis Khan. Frontier wars with Mamluk Egypt began, and there was also their eastern flank to contend with, where their cousins the Jagatai khans continually threatened to encroach on Iranian affairs. Even their own vassals, Afghans of the Kert family of Herat, made a stab at achieving independence and had to be besieged in 1307. It is therefore not surprising that the Ilkhans would pay little attention to north-west Anatolia, where a petty emirate of central Asian descent was behaving in a threatening fashion towards the Ilkhans' neighbours in the Byzantine Empire. At the request of the Byzantine emperor, Andronicus II, a force of Mongols intervened and were beaten by this new force – the Ottomans.

The above-mentioned khanate of Jagatai, Genghis Khan's second son, corresponded originally to the ancient kingdom of Kara-Khitai but, unlike Persia and China, the Jagatai khans had no conception of how to establish a regular state. They had none of the advantages enjoyed by their cousins in China and Persia who found at their disposal an age-old tradition of government into which they could enter as either Sultans or Sons of Heaven. The centre of the Jagatai khanate was a prairie, not a city, and the Jagatai khans remained both ignorant of urban life and aloof from it for far longer than their cousins. In fact the Khan Baraq, who reigned from 1266 to 1271, did not hesitate to order the pillage of Bukhara and Samarkand – his own cities – simply to obtain funds for the raising of an army.

The disintegration of the Jagatai khanate could therefore hardly be put down to effeminate urban living. The pillaging incidents at Bukhara and Samarkand came about because Baraq was opposed by Kaidu, a veteran of the great European campaign who had also challenged Khubilai for the

All that remains of the huge fortified caravanserai on the silk road between Bukhara and Samarkand. It was destroyed by the Mongols. (David Nicolle)

supreme khanship. Kaidu lived to a great age and was killed on active service in 1301, thus finally breaking the link with the Mongols of times past. During the 14th century the Jagatai khanate experienced turmoil until the old unity was restored under the forceful and dreaded khan, Tughlur Timur, but not many years were to pass before another Timur, known to history as Timur Lenk (Timur the Lame or 'Tamberlane'), was to replace the Jagatai khanate with an empire of his own.

Finally, a series of civil wars among the Mongols of the Golden Horde in the first half of the 14th century made the Russian princes suspect that their emperors had no clothes. From 1371 onwards the Russian princes ceased to render homage at the court of Sarai, or even to pay tribute. Grand Duke Dimitri of Moscow (later to receive the appellation of 'Dimitri of the Don') repulsed a punitive Mongol invasion in 1373 and hit back with

Grand Duke Dimitri of Moscow ('Dimitri of the Don') repulsed a Mongol invasion in 1373 and hit back with an advance of his own against Kazan in 1376. (Author's collection)

an advance of his own against Kazan in 1376. In 1378 he defeated a Mongol army for the first time and on 8 September 1380 he fought a second and more important battle at the field of Kulikovo, at the confluence of the Don and the Nepryadva.

The Russians were unable to capitalise on their victory owing to the intervention of Toqtamish, Khan of the White Horde, a separate minor khanate arising out of the division of territory among Jochi's sons. With the support of the growing power of Timur Lenk, Toqtamish brought the Russian princes back under Mongol control and ascended the throne of the Golden Horde. In 1382 Toqtamish invaded the Russian principalities and sacked the same towns that had suffered during the great invasion of Batu.

As the restorer of Mongol greatness, Toqtamish naturally felt that that he was called to follow in the footsteps of his ancestor, Genghis Khan, and it was no doubt with this in mind that he set about the conquest of Persia and central Asia. But Toqtamish was about 20 years too late because by 1387 these lands had already become the property of a leader of the first magnitude. The war that lasted between the two of them until 1397 ensured that the empire of the steppes did not stay with the ancient Mongol dynasty, but passed on to the new Turkic conqueror – Timur the Lame. A new era had begun.

The Mongol inheritance

Khubilai Khan had sent expeditions by land and sea to fight against war elephants, blowpipes and warriors running amok, and to experience the torments of jungle fighting and Japanese typhoons. His predecessors had faced the Russian winter and the desert sun of Palestine. Some of these operations may have ended in military failure or with a negotiated settlement, but the one sure success was what they all proved – that the Mongol army was able to learn from its experiences. Mongol aggression was never totally compromised by that peculiar military arrogance that has been the downfall of so many other military reputations. On the Russian steppes, outside Chinese walled towns, on Vietnamese rivers and in Indonesian jungles the Mongol armies demonstrated that their reputation for being somehow superhuman did not depend on mythical accounts of eternally galloping horsemen, but on something much more solid: the greatest example ever demonstrated of the ability to change.

Further reading

Grousset, Rene, *The Empire of the Steppes: A History of Central Asia* (1970).

Morgan, David, *The Mongols in Syria 1260–1300 in Edbury, P.W. (ed.) Crusade and Settlement (Cardiff 1985)*

Morgan, David, *The Mongols* (1986).

Smith, John Masson, 'Mongol Campaign Rations: Milk, marmots and blood?', *Journal of Mongolian Studies* 1996.

Turnbull, Stephen, Men-at-Arms 105: *The Mongols* (Oxford, Osprey Publishing, 1980).

Turnbull, Stephen, Warrior 84: *Mongol Warrior* (Oxford, Osprey Publishing, 2003).

Index

Visit the Osprey website

- Information about forthcoming books

- Author information

- Read extracts and see sample pages

- Sign up for our free newsletters

- Competitions and prizes